★ SAS AND ELITE FORC▓ ▓UIDE ★

CRISIS SU▓▓▓▓▓

**EARTHQUAKES, FLO▓ ▓SHES,
PAND▓▓**

★ SAS AND ELITE FORCES GUIDE ★
CRISIS SURVIVAL

EARTHQUAKES, FLOODS, FIRES, AIRPLANE CRASHES, PANDEMICS AND MANY MORE

ALEXANDER STILWELL

amber
BOOKS

First published in 2010 by
Amber Books Ltd
Bradley's Close
74–77 White Lion Street
London N1 9PF
www.amberbooks.co.uk

ISBN: 978-1-906626-82-2

Project Editor: Michael Spilling
Design: Graham Beehag
Illustrations: Tony Randell

Printed in Thailand

DISCLAIMER

This book is for information purposes only. Neither the author
or the publisher can accept responsibility for any loss, injury or
damage caused as a result of the use of the techniques described
in this book, nor for any prosecutions or proceedings brought
or instigated against any person or body that may result from
using these techniques.

CONTENTS

INTRODUCTION

Research has shown that you are most likely to survive a crisis or emergency if you are well prepared and if you act quickly and decisively. Although in the modern world we are used to many comforts and have many agencies and organizations that are equipped to minimize the effects of any crisis, you may still be confronted with a situation where the buck stops with you until professional help arrives. The crisis may be a fire in the home, a flood, a member of the family choking on food or a road rage incident. You may be out trekking and find yourself in trouble due to bad weather or an accident. There may be a major crisis such as a terrorist incident. In all of these cases, this book will help you to be prepared so that you can take action quickly when there is no time left to consider the options.

Flooding

Cars can be very easily swept away by flood water: just 60cm (2ft) of water can be enough to push a car along.

Preparation and equipment

There is a well-known phrase, 'A healthy mind in a healthy body'. You are more likely to cope with a crisis and achieve a successful outcome if you are both mentally and physically well prepared. This book reveals some techniques for preparing your mind and your body for the challenges of a crisis. The book also looks at first aid techniques which are fundamental to any accident or emergency, suggests what medical supplies you should carry and tells you how to treat a range of fractures and ailments. The equipment you

Life saving equipment

When undertaking any potentially dangerous activity, such as a sailing trip, it is essential to take along appropriate safety equipment, such as life jackets and floatation devices.

need for surviving a crisis in the home or that you should carry with you on an expedition is also described.

Survival techniques
The book discusses a range of natural disasters from floods to forest fires and helps you to prepare and survive. It also covers the complex nature of modern urban survival where the streets of a major city can be as dangerous as a jungle. Major accidents are covered, including what to do in a plane or train crash. The survival techniques for different regions of the world are also described and the book provides you with the essentials of navigation so that you can walk to safety. The book also analyses action to avoid or survive hostage-taking incidents.

Including a wide range of tips from top professional organizations and illustrated throughout, this book is your one-stop guide to preparing yourself for a crisis and surviving.

Vehicle hostage rescue

Anti-terrorist police may use a four-car box to trap a terrorist vehicle containing a hostage. If you are being held hostage, curl up on the seat or floor to give your rescuers clear lines of fire through the vehicle windows.

Basic first aid

Learning some basic first aid, such as how to treat a
sprained ankle, could save lives in a crisis situation.

The forces of nature are hugely powerful and often difficult to predict. Even in areas where certain kinds of natural disasters are relatively frequent, such as earthquakes and attendant tsunamis, warning systems are either poorly developed or do not exist at all. Forest fires can start and get out of control within a few hours. Tornados can travel as fast as a car and cause massive damage. Snow avalanches can occur in a split second on an otherwise serene mountainside.

In all these cases, however, you can greatly increase your chances of survival by being prepared and recognizing the warning signs and also by knowing what to do when the natural disaster is upon you.

Depending on which part of the world you live in, you may think that natural disasters happen somewhere else. Major flooding in the United Kingdom in 2007 was a reminder that natural disasters can strike anywhere, including temperate climate zones in northern Europe. Wherever you live, preparation is the key to surviving a crisis, and adequate preparation is made on the basis of good information. If you know the area

. . . .

Left: Natural disasters come in many forms and can strike at any time.

1

You can survive tsunamis, floods, fires, avalanches and hurricanes with proper preparation.

Crisis Situations
Surviving
Natural
Disasters

Taking cover

In very high winds, take refuge in a ditch or gully to avoid being blown across the ground or hit by flying debris.

you live in is in danger of a particular kind of natural disaster – flooding, forest fires, avalanches and so on – you can put in place precautions and develop an action plan. Once you have a plan, this can be put into action quickly if the disaster becomes imminent.

Apart from major natural disasters, other disasters can occur at any time within the context of the home, such as a fire caused by an electrical short circuit or a flare-up in the kitchen.

If you live in an area that is not in danger from the natural disasters listed in this section, make yourself aware of possible dangers in places you are planning to visit. If you plan to take part in a potentially dangerous sport, make sure you enrol on the appropriate training course. It may save your life.

HURRICANES AND TYPHOONS

Preparation for a hurricane

Hurricanes are unpredictable, so you need to be aware that high winds can pick up anything around the house that is loose and throw it against the house. First check that objects around the house are either secured or dismantled and put away in a store, such as a solid shed, or inside the house. Remember to put away children's play equipment, such as trampolines, climbing frames or slides.

Preparing your home

Cutting back branches near your house will help to protect it in high winds and minimize damage to your home.

How hurricanes form

Hurricanes or typhoons are usually formed in tropical oceans where the surface water is warm. Warm air spirals upwards in cyclonic winds and condenses.

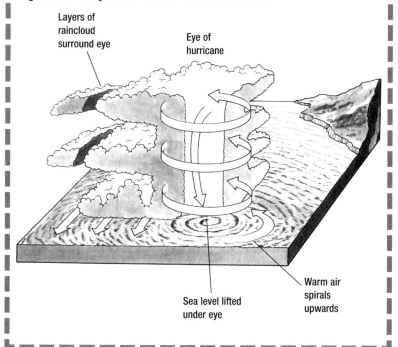

Layers of raincloud surround eye

Eye of hurricane

Sea level lifted under eye

Warm air spirals upwards

Make sure that all gutters and drains are cleared to allow water to flow away rapidly and without obstruction, so that it doesn't overflow out of drainpipes. If there are trees and shrubbery nearby, try to prune them back as far as possible to minimize the 'sail' effect in high winds, thereby reducing the risk of flying branches.

If you do not have shutters fitted to your windows, obtain some plywood and screw it over the window frames. Gather emergency supplies of tinned food and bottles of water. Ensure you have enough batteries to power torches, radios and other units, as well as candles and matches.

These destructive types of tropical cyclone are closely related. In the Atlantic and eastern Pacific, the term used is hurricane, whereas in the western Pacific they tend to be called typhoons. The winds travel at about 32m (105ft) per second and circle clockwise in the southern hemisphere and anti-clockwise in the northern hemisphere. At the centre (the 'eye') of the storm, there are only light breezes.

When a hurricane is forming, an area of low pressure is created at the surface as the storm rises. As the storm moves over the ocean, it picks up more warm moist air. The uptake of warm moist air creates more energy, which in turn creates stronger winds. The hurricane or typhoon will include devastating wind power and heavy rainfall, which normally strike twice at a single point – once as one 'wall' passes over, followed by relative calm as the eye of the storm moves across, followed by another wall of wind and rain, normally longer than the first.

Storm surge

The most dangerous aspect of the hurricane is known as the storm surge, which is caused by atmospheric pressure inside the hurricane sucking up the sea. Hurricane winds can cause large waves that hit the coastline, some of them up to 40ft (12m) high.

It is difficult to forecast a hurricane, but they are more likely to occur in the Atlantic region in August and September. A hurricane warning is normally issued at least 24–36 hours before a hurricane strikes. For actions in response to a hurricane, see earlier section on preparing the home.

TORNADOS

A tornado can be one of the most destructive natural events on earth. A full-size tornado can generate wind speeds of up to 500km/h (300mph), which are the fastest wind speeds on the planet. If a populated built-up area is hit by a major tornado, the results can be catastrophic.

Tornadoes can move across the ground at up to 48km/h (30mph) and sometimes up to 90km/h (55mph). This means they cannot be escaped on foot. A vehicle is a dangerous place in a tornado and your escape route may be blocked by traffic or other obstacles.

Fortunately, most tornadoes occur in deserted areas and many do not attain their full destructive potential.

Tornadoes are often formed during thunderstorms where polar air and tropical air meet.Tornados of varying sizes occur in many places, but by far the most

Formation of a tornado

Tornadoes are formed in areas where warm and cold air meet and there is a veering wind which may generate the spin effect that characterizes a tornado.

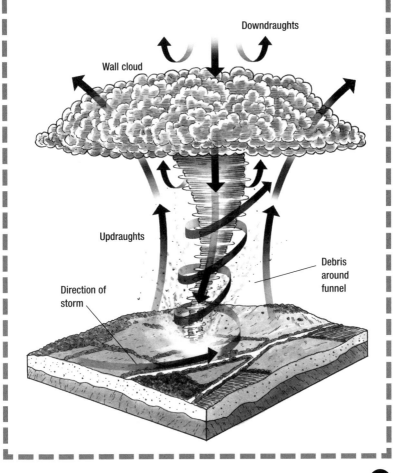

Downdraughts

Wall cloud

Updraughts

Debris around funnel

Direction of storm

Home provisions

If you are likely to be cut off by a natural disaster such as floods or deep snow, keep a supply of essential food and equipment.

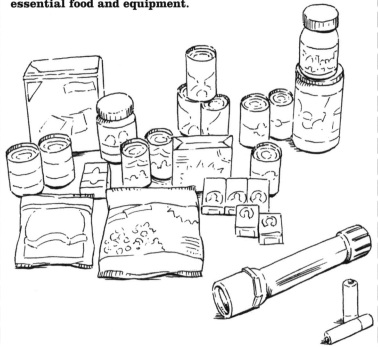

significant area for tornados of a destructive variety in the northern hemisphere is the United States, followed by Canada. In the southern hemisphere, they occur in Australia as well as in South America.

Tornado damage
Human fatalities and injuries
In the United States, tornados cause more than 80 fatalities per year. Deaths and injuries in tornados have a number of causes, including flying debris, violent falls and being sucked

up into the vortex of the tornado and then falling.

Damage to buildings
Tornados have a massively destructive effect on buildings. The vortex effect of the wind can pull roofs off buildings and it pulls windows and doors outwards. If wind gets inside the building, the effect is exacerbated.

Surviving a tornado
Inside
If you see a tornado approaching, suspect one may be imminent due to prevailing weather conditions, or have received a tornado warning, the priority is to take shelter in a secure part of the house, having made sure that all doors and windows and shutters are securely fastened. If you are in a poorly constructed building, a mobile home or caravan, move to a sturdy building or take refuge outside in a secure area.

The safest place indoors in a tornado is a basement or cellar or in a small room without windows, such as a downstairs lavatory or utility area. Stay well clear of windows, as these are easily shattered in a tornado that will send shards of glass flying at high speed.

Another place to take refuge is under a sturdy table. You can use mattresses, blankets and thick clothing for extra protection. Put your arms around your neck and head to protect them.

Outside
If a tornado is approaching when you are outside, try to keep low on the ground and if possible hold on to something immovable. Try to get into a ditch or under a strong covered area such as a culvert.

If you are in a car, be advised that this is not a safe place. Powerful tornados can roll cars over or even suck them up into the air and drop them. If you are in a car, get out and try to find a safe place, as indicated in the paragraph above.

FLOODS
Flooding is most common around coastal areas, river deltas and estuaries. Due to housing pressure, houses are sometimes now built on flood plains, making them susceptible to flooding from swollen rivers during freak rainstorms.

After normal rainfall, water is absorbed by the soil and vegetation, and some of it disappears through evaporation. The remainder, known as the run-off, flows into streams and rivers. Under normal conditions, streams and rivers can usually absorb the extra capacity. When the rain is particularly severe and continuous, the water level rises, rivers burst their banks and the water overlows onto the land around it.

Another flood factor in urban environments is that natural earth drainage is scarce, due to tarmac roads and concrete car parking areas and so on, so the water has nowhere to settle and be absorbed into the ground. Drains are designed for a reasonable capacity of water, but often cannot cope with the volume of water that results from continuous rain over a long period, as there is not enough time for drainage to take place. Sometimes in a storm, leaves and mud block drains, which makes the problem worse. (See above for preparations for a flood in your home and how to seal your house.)

If you are outside and caught in a flood, or if a flood is imminent, make your way to high ground as soon as possible. Do not try to wade through the flood. The current is likely to be too powerful and there may be dangerous objects floating about.

Preparation for a flood

Research about the level of danger from flooding for your area. You can normally find this out through government information websites. The likelihood of your house being flooded will depend on what level you live on geographically. You are obviously less likely to be flooded if you live on a hill, though people who live on hills can be affected by water coursing down the hill and flowing out of drains.

If a flood warning has been issued, or if you can see that flooding is likely in your area, give yourself plenty of time to move valuables from the bottom floor of your house to a higher floor – items including furniture, rugs, ornaments, and electronic equipment.

Make sure you know how to turn off main energy supplies, including electricity and gas. Prepare

Dinghy

A tough rubber dinghy with oars is a useful standby if you live in a flood danger area.

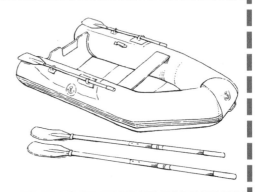

emergency supplies in a safe part of the house, to include torches and lamps, spare food and water, a radio (for information), telephones and a first aid kit.

Sandbags

Use sandbags to block vital entrances into your house. Depending on the design of your house and garden, you may want to place an outer defence round a garden gate, but take note that in some countries free sandbags will not be supplied to protect gardens.

In an emergency, the supply of sandbags will probably be limited, so it is wise either to buy your own or make up your own by filling bags with earth or gravel from the garden.

Sealing your home

Sealing your home effectively from flooding will take some time and require early warning of impending floods.

TIP:
ADDITIONAL FLOODING PROTECTION

In addition to sandbags, there are other ways of protecting your home from water.

- You can obtain air brick covers to stop water seeping through these bricks, which are designed to provide ventilation.
- You can place fitted door guards across the entrances to your house, which can be kept in place by sandbags.
- Water can sometimes enter a house by backing up the drains (which can be very unpleasant). You can have non-return valves fitted to drains and water-inlet valves.
- If you live in a high flood-risk area, you may want to consider moving your electrical sockets to a metre or so above floor level.
- If you are re-decorating your house, consider putting hard floors on the ground floor and using rugs instead of carpets. You can move the rugs more easily if there is a risk of flood and you can clean hard floors more easily cleaned than fitted carpets.

Sandbags will slow down the ingress of water, but they will not provide a guaranteed watertight seal. Filling and moving sandbags is hard work, so make your preparations well in advance and keep up to date with weather warnings.

At least six sandbags will be required to protect a standard door opening from 20cm (7.8in) of water depth. You can improve the seal against the door by using a heavy duty PVC plastic sheet. When arranging the bags in front of an entrance, follow the pattern of a brick wall, i.e. the second layer should overlap the meeting point between the two bags below (see diagram page 21). Firm the bags down so they are as closely welded together as possible.

Do not build the sandbag wall too high, as this could become unstable and dangerous. If you intend to build a sandbag wall more than three layers high, you should construct a

Seeking higher ground

In severe flooding, you may need to plan an escape route onto the roof of your house or to higher ground.

TIP:
DRIVING IN FLOODED AREAS

If a flood is imminent, move your car to higher ground.
Do not attempt to drive through a flood unless absolutely
necessary.

- Do not attempt to drive through standing water unless you
  know how deep it is. If your engine is swamped with water, it
  may cut out. If the water is very deep, the vehicle may start
  to float and you may become stranded.
- If you have to negotiate a flood that you judge is not too deep
  for your vehicle, drive slowly and steadily so that you do not
  create a bow wave and swamp the engine.
- Do not attempt to drive through a flood if a vehicle is coming
  the other way, as the wave effect from the other car may
  swamp your engine.
- Keep a set of emergency equipment (see below) in your car in
  case you become stranded: blanket, torch, first aid kit, spare
  water, food, mobile telephone.

First aid kit

Jump leads

Tow rope

Blanket

Windscreen
wiper

pyramid wall in which the width is three times the height of the wall. This will require a large number of bags (see diagram page 157). For extra protection, add a waterproof PVC sheet to the outside of the wall, weighing it down with bags.

TSUNAMIS

A tsunami is an extreme tidal wave caused by an earthquake or similar geological disturbance. Tsunamis are rare in many parts of the world, but in freak conditions they can extend themselves to affect a wide area. In December 2004, a megathrust earthquake off Sumatra created a series of devastating tsunamis that affected 11 nations and killed 230,000 people.

Tsunamis are extremely dangerous for a number of reasons. Although generally caused by earthquakes, the maritime earthquake may not be apparent to anyone on the surface without appropriate measuring equipment, and at sea the initial tsunami wave may be almost unnoticeable as it moves towards the land.

Tsunami waves are known to have passed by ships at sea at a height of only 3ft (1m). By the time they reach the coast, however, an average tsunami may have grown to a height of 15m (50ft). The tsunami waves that struck around the Indian Ocean in 2004, however, reached heights of 30m (100ft), making them some of the largest and most devastating tsunami waves in history.

Apart from the difficulty of spotting tsunami waves at sea and therefore providing early warning, as well as the challenges of detecting the initial earthquake, the other lethal characteristic of a tsunami is its speed. At sea, a tsunami wave may travel at a speed of 500–1000km/h (310–620mph). When it reaches the shore, the wave slows down comparatively, but is still travelling at about 80km/h (50mph). Even if it is spotted as it approaches, people have very little chance of escaping by foot.

Early warning signs of a tsunami

In the 2004 tsunami disaster, some people took early evasive action, and helped others to safety, because they recognized the early signs of a tsunami. The sea at the shoreline sometimes draws back abnormally (there may be a sucking sound and frothing bubbles), exposing areas of the beach/ocean bed that are usually under water. (At Kalutara, Sri Lanka, in 2004, the sea receded dramatically before the tsunami struck.) If this happens, raise the alarm and move to high ground or to a high building. Tell everyone urgently to do the same. In 2004, at least 100 people were saved from the tsunami by a 10-year-old English

How tsunamis work

A tsunami is often triggered by an undersea earthquake. Seismic sea waves then travel inland to cause huge destruction in coastal areas.

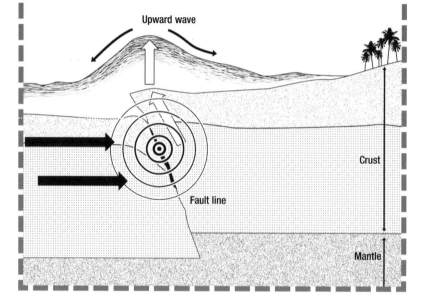

Upward wave

Crust

Fault line

Mantle

girl – and indirectly by her geography teacher. The girl had learned in school about the early signs of a tsunami, including the receding sea, and had enough presence of mind to warn her parents and everyone around them. They escaped to higher ground and survived.

Sometimes, unusual behaviour by animals can be the sign of an impending tsunami. Some species of animal are thought to be able to hear the earthquake, and they move inland to higher ground.

If you are living in or visiting an area that is known to have suffered tsunamis in the past, such as countries around the Indian Ocean, keep abreast of weather reports and any information that might filter through from earthquake early-

Tidal surge

Storm surges happen when tropical cyclones cause an offshore rise of water. High winds push on the ocean's surface, causing the water to pile up higher than the ordinary sea level. The sudden rise in water level can create tidal waves that flood coastal areas.

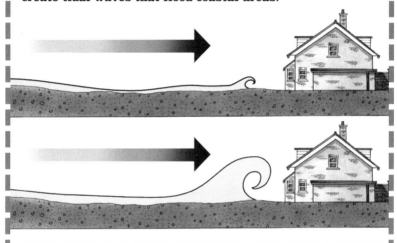

warning systems. Be aware of the warning signs of tsunamis and work out an escape route, which will be signposted in some high-risk areas. Leave the coastline immediately if you have any suspicion something may be wrong.

Be aware of the geography of the place you live in or are visiting. Where would you go if a tsunami struck and you needed to find refuge from the flood? There are too many videos of the 2004 tsunami taken by people who were obviously not aware of the significance of the huge white wall of water extending across the horizon and coming inland towards them like an express train. People continued to look out to sea and ask themselves what that sight might be. Little children continued to play on the beach while the wall of water approached.

Drowning victim

Quick action can save a drowning person, though take care when carrying out a rescue.

Tsunami action
- Call the alarm
- Warn everyone to move
- Take your companions with you
- Get away fast to high ground or into a strong, high building.

EARTHQUAKES

Earthquakes are some of the most destructive natural phenomena on earth and also have equally destructive side-effects, such as tsunamis (see above). As with tsunamis, earthquakes can in theory occur anywhere in the world but they are more likely to occur in areas where separate tectonic plates come together, and it is here that they will have the most destructive effects. There is an earthquake belt around the Pacific Ocean that affects countries such as New Zealand and Japan, New Guinea and the western coasts of North and South America. Another belt runs from the Mediterranean through to Indonesia via Asia.

Side effects

Most earthquakes occur when the tectonic plates either slide against each other or pass over or under each other. Some earthquakes, however, do not occur at the edges of plates. Some conditions make the effects of earthquakes worse, including mud and clay soils and water-logged low-lying regions. Apart from waves such as tsunamis, earthquakes can also trigger landslides. After the main earthquake shock, there is often a series of aftershocks caused by the knock-on effect of the released energy underground. The frequency of the aftershocks is in inverse proportion to the length of time after the original earthquake. You should therefore be prepared for further, though less serious, disturbances.

Earthquake hazards

The biggest danger to humans from earthquakes (apart from side effects such as tsunamis, landslides and fires) is their effect on man-made structures such as houses, office blocks, roads, bridges and so on. Often such man-made buildings are not constructed to withstand the vibration of an earthquake and therefore collapse.

Action to take in an earthquake
Indoors
- If you are inside a building, get under a strong table or other form of overhead protection to shield yourself from falling masonry and

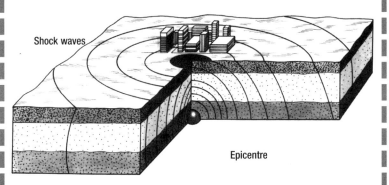

Epicentre of an earthquake

An initial earthquake will often be followed by aftershocks as energy is released underground.

Shock waves

Epicentre

objects. Stay under cover as long as the tremors continue.

- If there is no obvious protection to get under, place yourself as close as possible to an inside wall. Keep away from windows and any other glass that might shatter.

- Door frames are another place you can stand under for better protection.
- Do not use lift/elevators.
- Do not attempt to run out of a building during an earthquake, as you will be at risk of injury from falling and flying objects.

Preparing for an earthquake

Avoid leaving large items of unstable furniture near key exits in your home, impeding a rescue or escape routes.

Outside

- Do not attempt to run away from an earthquake, as it is difficult to pinpoint where its main effect lies and you are likely to run into more danger.
- Keep away from trees, buildings or any other structures that might fall on you.
- Keep clear of telephone poles, electricity pylons and any other wires. Never try to touch or move any cable that has fallen.

Vehicle

If you are driving a vehicle, slow down and if possible drive to a clear space as far as possible from

Duck, cover and hold

Find a secure place to take cover in an earthquake, such as under a sturdy table in the centre of your house.

Home survival kit

Emergency supplies may include a radio to keep up with emergency reports and a first aid kit.

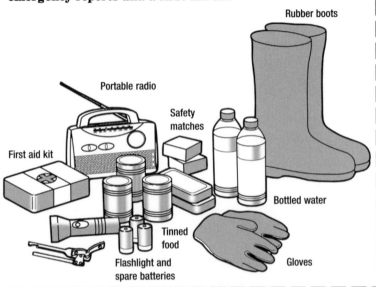

Rubber boots

Portable radio

Safety matches

First aid kit

Bottled water

Tinned food

Flashlight and spare batteries

Gloves

The Richter Scale	
Force of Earthquake	**Scale**
Not felt but recorded on seismometer	2.6
Widely felt	3.5
Local damage	4.5
Destructive earthquake	6.0
Major earthquake	7.0
Great earthquake	8.0+

The Mercali Scale	
I.	Felt by almost no one.
II.	Felt by very few people.
III.	Tremor noticed, but not recognized as an earthquake.
IV.	Felt indoors by many.
V.	Felt by almost everyone. Trees and poles swaying.
VI.	Felt by everyone. Furniture moved. Slight damage.
VII.	Everyone runs outdoors. Considerable damage to poorly built structures.
VIII.	Specially designed structures damaged; others collapse.
IX.	All buildings considerably damaged. Cracks in ground.
X.	Many structures destroyed. Ground badly cracked.
XI.	All structures fall. Bridges wrecked. Wide cracks in the ground.
XII.	Total destruction. Waves seen on ground.

underpasses, lamp posts or trees. Do not panic, as you could cause an accident. Stay in the vehicle until the shaking stops.

At home

If you live in an earthquake region, or if you are visiting an earthquake region for a period of time, make sure you inform yourself of any advance warning systems (including knowing which radio stations to tune into) and also any local shelters. Find out the phone numbers for local emergency services. Make a plan with family and friends as to where you will meet in an emergency and where the safest place is to be in an earthquake. Assemble an emergency kit, which should include:

- First aid kit
- Flashlight and spare batteries
- Candles and matches
- Spare food and water
- A radio
- Telephones (preferably mobiles)

Educate yourself and family and friends of possible earthquake early-warning signs, such as:

- Unusual behaviour by animals – dogs behaving strangely, strange bird calls at night and so on.
- Sudden changes of water levels

in wells or artesian bores can be a sign of an impending earthquake.

Action after an earthquake

Turn off energy supplies and do not light matches until you have checked for gas leaks.

Check people for injuries and give first aid where necessary. Use the telephone only in an emergency, and use your radio to keep informed. Check the area you are in for signs of weakened structures, such as cracks and asymmetrical buildings.

If the building you are in is severely damaged, move somewhere else, but be prepared for the secondary shocks that often follow the main earthquake. Do not use a vehicle unless absolutely necessary.

VOLCANOES

A volcano is caused by a vent in the earth's crust which allows molten rock and other material to escape from super-heated parts of the earth's core.

Volcanoes are often associated with the movement of the world's tectonic plates and therefore the likelihood of their occurrence is often associated with the margins of these plates where they rub together. Volcanoes are characterized according to the degree of explosiveness on an increasing scale:

• Icelandic
• Hawaiian
• Strombolian
• Vulcanian
• Pelican
• Plinian

Active volcanoes are closely monitored and it is likely that warnings of volcanic activity will be given in good time. If you are visiting an area with a history of volcanic activity, make sure you have the latest update on activity and also find out what the emergency arrangements are.

Depending on the type of volcano, there are a range of potential dangers. During an eruption, lava and steam are thrown out of the volcano. This may also include large pieces of rock and other material. Rocks weighing up to 8 tonnes can be thrown over a distance of 5km (3 miles). If a volcano is erupting and throwing out missiles of this kind, it is essential that you have either taken measures to get out of range of the volcano or identified a secure shelter, preferably on high ground to avoid the dangers of lava flow.

Some lava is slow-moving and can be avoided. On steep slopes, however, it can move faster than a person can run. Volcanoes also throw out ash which can crush buildings if it builds up. Wear protective goggles and some form of breathing protection, which may be either a mask or a damp cloth.

Volcanoes

Volcanic erruptions occur in many different types. Some will simply ooze slow-moving lava (B), while others will detonate with a huge explosion (A).

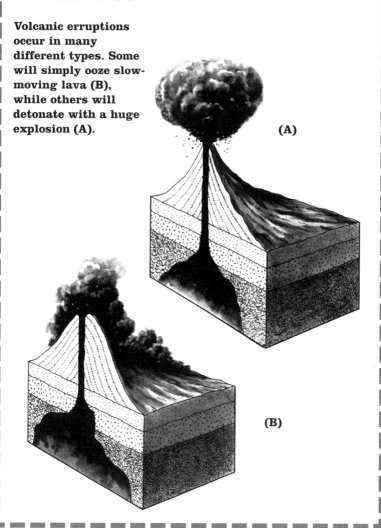

(A)

(B)

STORMS AND BLIZZARDS

These severe natural phenomena strike all too frequently in winter months across cold areas of the world. In the United States, a 'snowbelt' extends across the Great Lakes region from Minnesota to Maine. Cities affected include Buffalo, New York City, Milwaukee and Detroit. A snow blizzard can strike like lightning and have astonishing force. The blizzards in the US snowbelt are generally much more severe than those experienced in Europe.

If a snowstorm is imminent, it is best to stay inside if at all possible and to wait for the storm to die down. Deaths or injuries in snowstorms and blizzards can be caused by a number of reasons, both direct and indirect. People can be cut off in snowstorms if they are out on foot or in cars and succumb to hypothermia and starvation. Vehicles

Blizzard-bound

If you are stuck in your car during a blizzard, stay with the vehicle:

- Keep the window open a crack for air.
- Stay warm by moving your arms and legs to keep the blood flowing.
- Start the car engine once every hour and use the heater for ten minutes to keep the vehicle functioning.
- Keep the exhaust pipe clear so that fumes can escape.

TIP:
PREPARING FOR A SNOW STORM

When you know a snow storm is coming, you should take the following action to safeguard yourself and your home:

- Try to stay inside if possible, but if you have to go outdoors, prepare yourself against the cold.
- Check the insulation around exterior pipes.
- Wear lots of layers – a few lightweight layers give more warmth than a single heavy coat.
- Find out the wind chill factor, because wind and cold can drive down your body temperature.
- Take care when walking on icy sidewalks and snow. Wear hiking or snow boots.
- Always tell someone where you are going, how you are getting there, and when you think you will arrive.
- Try not to drive, but keep the tank full and the fuel line from freezing.
- Prepare your car for winter cold and snow – flush the radiator and buy antifreeze. Make sure the headlights are working properly.
- Check and refill your heating fuel supply. Stock up on firewood if necessary.
- Inside your house, store emergency food and water and other necessary supplies.
- Clean out the chimney flue to prevent fire hazard.
- Conserve heat by closing doors or heating only essential rooms.
- Stuff rolled blankets or towels under doors and cracks to block draughts.

TIP: AVOIDING LIGHTNING STRIKES

- Avoid making yourself the tallest object or standing near the tallest object in your immediate area.
- Avoid potential conductors such as wire, metal and water.
- Get into a building or car if a lightning strike is possible.
- Stand away from others to avoid conduction through the group if anyone is struck.
- Avoid using the telephone, electrical appliances or metal objects such as ladders and taps (faucets).
- If you feel your hair stand on end – the indicator of an imminent lightning strike – jump into a shelter or drop to a crouching position straight away, keeping as low to the ground as you possibly can.

can slide off roads, causing accidents.

At home

If you live in a snow-prone area, make sure your house is well prepared and stocked up with emergency supplies in case you are cut off by the snow. If fuel supplies are likely to be cut off, ensure you have enough alternative supplies, such as wood or coal. A good supply of tinned food should be kept in reserve as well as other food supplies. Insulate your house with double glazing and use weather strips where appropriate. Temporary plastic double-glazing can be used where necessary. Pipes should be insulated and a boiler may be fitted with a cold-weather monitor to avoid freezing pipes.

Rain storms

Rain storms can be equally dangerous, causing both hazards on the roads and damage to your home. In these conditions lightning strikes are common. Never take refuge under a tree or other tall structure during a heavy storm, since such features attract lightning strikes.

Outdoors

If you are outdoors during a snowstorm or blizzard, beware extreme exertion such as shovelling snow or attempting to free trapped vehicles as this can lead to heart

Thunder and lightning

When lightning is close, crouch down and minimize the number of contact points with the ground.

failure, depending on your age and level of fitness, and/or muscle strain. If you are wearing thick winter clothing, you may be in danger of losing too much body fluid through excessive sweating.

Also, if you sweat into your clothes you will make them wet which raises the risk of hypothermia. Extremely cold air can affect the lungs so cover your mouth with a scarf or other headwear. Beware the risk of frostbite, especially in your extremities such as fingers or toes.

Vehicles in a snowstorm

If you are stuck in a vehicle in a snowstorm, it is best to either remain in or near the vehicle until help arrives. Take care to clear snow away from near the exhaust pipe to reduce the risk of carbon monoxide poisoning and turn the engine on for a short period at least once every hour to provide warmth. It may be necessary to keep one window slightly open to avoid bad air or the dangers of carbon monoxide. Go through a periodic regime of

TIP:
VEHICLE PREPARATION

If you are travelling in or live in an area prone to snowstorms, it is a good idea to keep emergency supplies constantly in the vehicle. These may include:

- A shovel.
- Windscreen ice/snow scrapers.
- Torch and spare batteries.
- Water.
- Spare food, including energy bars.
- Candles and matches.
- First aid kit.
- Blankets/spare thermal/waterproof clothing.
- Flares and other distress signals.
- Rope or chain strong enough to tow a vehicle.
- Rock salt and/or sand may be carried to improve traction. Tyre chains may be appropriate.
- Plastic bags for rubbish or hygiene requirements.

Preparing your car

- Remember to make sure your have a full tank of petrol if venturing onto the road in extreme weather conditions. You never know how long your journey might take, or whether you will be stuck somewhere.

- You should always keep the following items in your car in storm and blizzard conditions: bottled water, blankets, winter coat, gloves, hat, shovel, rope, tire chains and a flashlight.

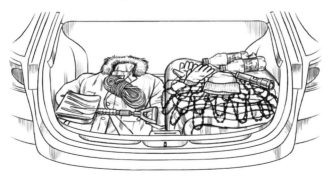

exercises to keep warm and make use of any blankets and clothing that may be available.

It goes without saying that you should prepare your car in case of a possible emergency and keep it properly serviced. Apart from the use of flares or a bright piece of cloth attached to an aerial, you can put the car bonnet up to attract attention as long as there is no danger of the engine being affected by falling snow.

AVALANCHES

There are various kinds of avalanches, though they have in

Avalanche

There are many different types of avalanche structure, but you should be especially cautious about overhanging slabs of wet snow that have the wind behind them.

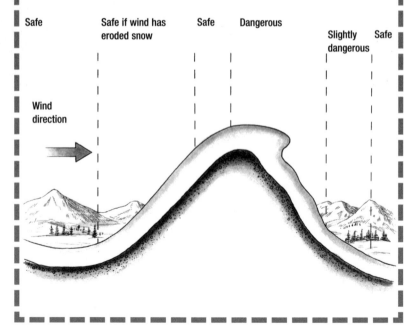

Safe   Safe if wind has eroded snow   Safe   Dangerous   Slightly dangerous   Safe

Wind direction

TIP:
AVOIDING SNOW AVALANCHES

- Be aware of the snow conditions mentioned above and take advice from an expert guide.
- Look for signs of where previous avalanches have occurred. Avalanches tend to occur in the same areas.
- Look for obvious signs, such as cracks appearing in the snow and pieces of snow beginning to tumble downhill.
- Beware if the snow sounds hollow underneath.
- If you are crossing an avalanche danger area, make sure you are roped together with your team mates and that you move as far up the hill as possible.
- When moving, keep an eye out for solid objects against which you can anchor yourself, such as rocks or trees.
- Take a slope meter with you. This device allows you to measure the gradient of a slope so that you know whether you are in the 30–50° danger area.
- Wear a helmet and carry a safety beacon, shovel and probe pole.

common the movement of loose or recently detached snow down a sloping area. The avalanche can contain rock, debris or ice, and they are a lethal phenomenon – due to their frequency, snow avalanches cause the deaths of at least 150 people a year in North America and Europe.

Due to the delicate nature of snow and the large quantities in which it gathers, snow avalanches can be triggered by movement across danger areas.

A slab avalanche (a large section of snow breaking off and sliding down a hill) occurs where the gradient of the slope is between 30° and 50° and there are no obstacles to anchor the snow, such as trees or protruding rocks. Heavy snowfall, high winds, rain and rising temperatures can trigger slab avalanches.

In winter, the north slope of a snow-covered mountain is more likely to experience an avalanche than the south slope; in summer, it is the south slope that is the dangerous

TIP:
HOW TO RESCUE SOMEONE CAUGHT
IN AN AVALANCHE

- If your partner is caught in an avalanche, you will not have time to get help. Time is limited and you have to search yourself before they suffocate under the snow.
- Watch the victim closely as they fall and try to work out his likely position based on where you last saw him.
- Check that the avalanche is completely over before you attempt to help.
- If there is more than one of you, make a logical and systematic search plan to cover the entire area.
- Use a rescue beacon if you have one (this requires careful reading of the manufacturers' instructions and practice).
- Use your probe before you dig, probing through the snow gently but firmly in an attempt to locate the casualty.

area. The leeward slope of a hill (the opposite to windward) is generally more dangerous because the wind will have blown the snow into drifts there. A cornice is an overhanging mass of snow that forms on the crest of a ridge; this may break off, and if it does, this is likely to trigger an avalanche.

Surviving avalanches
If you are caught in an avalanche, try to throw off any heavy equipment you may be wearing, such as a backpack or skis – heavy equipment pulls you downwards so you are likely to end up deeper in the snow. If you are skiing or snowboarding, try to keep the momentum going and steer towards the edge of the avalanche. Deploy any safety equipment you may be carrying, such as a breathing lung or inflatable bag.

When the snow hits, try to work your way to the side of the avalanche by using a backstroke motion, keeping your face upwards to breathe. As the avalanche slows, try to force a hand or leg through to the surface and keep a hand in front of your face for air.

LANDSLIDES

Landslides can occur almost anywhere there is a slope. A landslide can have a number of causes, including severe rainfall, earthquakes and poor land use, such as deforestation. A landslide consists of a mixture of earth, rocks and water which moves rapidly down a slope and then picks up other objects on its way, including trees and cars.

If you are in an area where there is a danger of landslides, get the latest updates and hazard assessments. If a landslide is imminent, you may notice cracks appearing in or around the house, doors sticking as frames move, the movement of fences or

Surviving an avalanche

If caught in an avalanche, try to remain as close to the surface as possible, using a backstroke swimming action.

Landslides and slumps

A slump is caused when a chunk of land loosens (often following the effects of rainfall) and drops. Landslides occur when pieces of land break away from the mass.

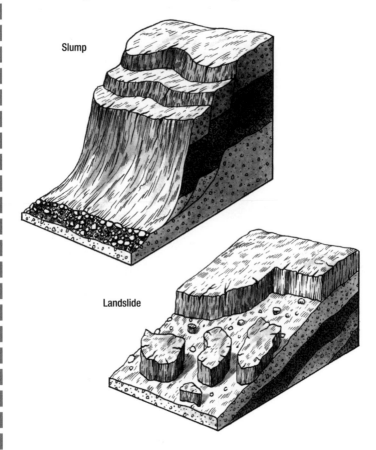

Slump

Landslide

Mudslides and rockfalls

Mudslides are often caused by extremely heavy rainfall, after loose earth has become saturated with rain water. Rockfalls occur when when bits of rock loosen and break away in areas of structural weakness.

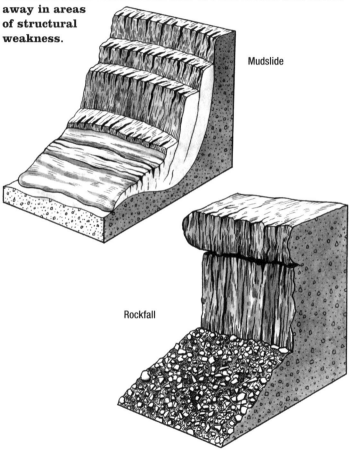

Mudslide

Rockfall

walls and also a rumbling sound. Water may appear in unexpected places and river water may become brown with mud.

What to do in a landslide

If a landslide is imminent or already beginning, you must get out of the path of the landslide as soon as possible. Do not attempt to take belongings as this will delay your escape. If you have time, contact the local rescue services and also any neighbours who may be in danger.

The priority is to get out of the path of the landslide and/or to get on to higher ground which is not at risk. If you are in a car and the embankment begins to give way, you need to stop and get out or return in the direction you came, while if you are in a building and do not have time to get away, find a secure area, such as under a sturdy table, keep your head down and hold on. If you are caught in a landslide, there is little you can do except curl up in a ball and protect your head with your hands.

You should not return to the area of a landslide until there is full official clearance as to safety as there may be secondary landslides after the major one and the ground may remain unstable. There may also be other hazards such as fallen power lines which can kill instantly if touched. There may be broken gas mains or potential floods from fractured water mains or overflowing rivers. Burst sewage pipes and toxic materials may contaminate the water so take care to use bottled water or other secure supplies until the area is cleared. Animals can become scared and therefore dangerous in these conditions.

FIRES AND WILDFIRES

Home fires

Fires are a common hazard and can lead to thousands of deaths per year. Many of the deaths are caused by the asphyxiating effect of heavy smoke rather than by burns. As a basic precaution, do not leave anything flammable hanging near a heat source such as an open fire or electric fire.

Fire warning in the house is best achieved through the installation of smoke alarms in key areas, such as in the passages outside bedrooms, at the top of stairwells and within reasonable range of the kitchen. Do not place them in areas where they will receive direct heat from other sources such as light bulbs as they will then become an annoyance and there is a danger that they will be ignored in a real emergency. Fire alarms should be periodically cleaned and checked for battery life.

Another part of fire defence is planning an escape route with all members of the family (see diagram, pages 50–51). As with any emergency, there is little time to think in a fire and family members need to know where to go in the dark. In case the lights fail, equip each family member with a torch.

When planning escape routes, you need to take into account whether windows can be fully opened or have bars across them (for example, child safety bars). If windows or doors have security locks, ensure keys are easily accessible. If you may need to jump out of a particular window, check that the ground remains clear underneath.

Hazards may include stakes (cane or metal) that are put in the ground to support plants. Remove them and find other ways of supporting the plants. Take account of any fences or railings. It may be possible to throw a mattress out to cushion a

Home fire

- **When moving around the house in a fire, stay close to the ground to avoid the smoke.**
- **Before opening a door, place the back of your hand against the exit to see if it is hot. This will tell you whether the fire is raging the other side.**

Knowing your escape routes

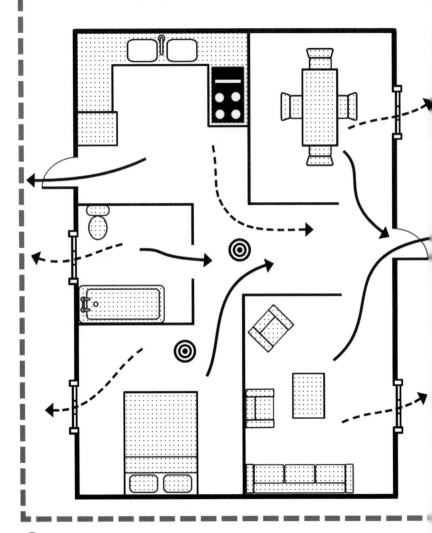

- Have fire drills with your family on a regular basis. Obtain a map of the area surrounding your home. Review the map and plot two or more evacuation routes that you may use when fleeing a fire.

- If a wildfire is threatening your area, listen to your radio for updated reports and evacuation information. If advised to evacuate, do so immediately.

- Wear protective clothing and footwear to protect yourself from flying sparks and ashes.

- Prepare an evacuation pack that you can pick up at a moment's notice. It should include: drinking water, a change of clothes and footwear, a blanket or sleeping bag for each person, a first aid kit (with any prescription medication), emergency tools, a battery-powered flashlight and radio, extra sets of keys, credit cards and cash.

PRIMARY EXIT
———————————➤

ALTERNATIVE EXIT
- - - - - - - - - - - - ➤

SMOKE ALARM

Forest fires – how to prepare your home

Wildfires can strike at any time, and affect even urban areas, as fires in California and Australia have shown in recent years. People in fire prone areas should plan ahead and be prepared to evacuate with little notice. There are many things you can do to protect yourself and your property.

- Make a fire safe zone around your house. Remove combustibles, including firewood, yard waste, barbecue grills, and fuel cans, from an area at least nine metres (30 feet) around the house and any outbuildings.

- **Prune away the lower limbs of evergreens that are within the fire safe zone.**
- **Remove any branches that overhang the roof or chimney and remove leaves and needles from gutters.**
- **Hose with water any wooden areas around the outside of your house, such as fences, trellises and outbuildings. If it is made of wood, also hose down the roof.**
- **Cover vents, windows and other openings of the house with duct tape and pieces of plywood.**
- **Shut off natural gas, propane or fuel oil supplies.**
- **Inside the house, move combustible materials such as light curtains and furniture away from the windows.**
- **Fill any large vessels – such as a swimming pool, hot tub or garbage cans – with water to slow or discourage fire.**
- **Make sure firefighters can find and access your home; mark your house and local roads clearly.**

fall. Check the window aperture is wide enough. It may be possible to keep a ladder inside the house that can be lowered through an appropriate window.

When moving around the house in a fire, stay close to the ground where the air is likely to be clearer. Before leaving a room, place the back of your hand against the door to see if it is hot. If it is hot, it is probably too dangerous to open the door and you may need to attempt an escape out of the window or signal for rescue. If the door is cool, try opening it slowly to check conditions outside, and then move out if safe, following your agreed escape route or towards where family members or rescuers may call you.

Outdoors

Fires outdoors often occur in the summer, when dry foliage and forest debris can easily catch fire. In Australia, the eucalyptus tree drops a great deal of dry bark and leaves on the forest floor, which together makes ready fuel. Fires can also occur in brushland and grassland.

Prevention

Take great care when lighting a camp fire, especially in a dry area – use a constructed fireplace or light the fire in a trench at least 30cm (12in) deep. Take care that roots

TIP:
ACTION IF CAUGHT IN A FIRE

- Try to take refuge in a pond, lake or river if possible.
- Look for shelter in a clear area or among rocks.
- Lie flat and cover your body and head with wet clothing or with soil.
- Breathe air close to the ground to avoid scorching your lungs or inhaling smoke.
- If the flames are quite low and you can see a burnt patch beyond the flames, you can attempt to dash through the flames to the burnt area.
- If you decide to dash to safety, cover as much of the surface of your body as possible and dampen clothes and hair if you have water.
- If your clothes catch fire, do not stay on your feet once out of the fire, but crouch down or roll to smother the flames.
- A fire is totally unpredictable and will change direction rapidly according to the wind. Be aware of the wind direction.

near the fire do not catch alight or that any loose material on the fire blows away. Clear the ground at least 3m (10ft) around the camp fire. Do not light a fire when conditions are hot and windy and when the bush is dry. If a fire starts, use a branch with green leaves to try to smother it or use fire-fighting equipment that may be available, such as poles with beating flaps on the end.

Wildfires

Wildfires are a major threat especially in summer in areas where there has been a shortage of rainfall. It is very easy to start a wildfire – a discarded cigarette butt or a piece of glass focussing the sun's rays can do it – but they are very difficult to control once they have grown.

In order to protect your home, create a 9m (30ft) safety zone around it so that any fire will have less

Clothing on fire

If your clothing catches fire, smother the flames immediately by falling to the floor and rolling over.

chance of reaching the building. Cut down any vegetation, especially dry vegetation and also clear any dry leaves off the lawn. Keep the lawn itself trimmed.

DROUGHTS AND HEATWAVES

It may come as a surprise that droughts affect more people than any other natural hazard. In the United States, droughts have been known to extend all the way from New England to Florida and the Ohio Valley as well as across the Western States. Major droughts mostly occur at latitudes of about 15–20° in areas which border on permanently dry areas, such as deserts. In Africa, rainfall can vary widely within a season and be very localized when it falls. In order to mitigate the affects of drought, national and state organizations need to coordinate and preserve water resources efficiently. A common sign of water shortage is a hose-pipe ban.

If you have experienced protracted dry conditions and there are official warnings of drought conditions, take care to store enough bottled water in a cool and secure area. The average requirement for each person should be measured as about 4.5 litres (1.2 gallons) of water per person per day.

In an emergency, water can be taken from other locations, such as the house water-tank and boiled before drinking. Ice from the freezer can also be melted and boiled.

Dos and don'ts in a drought

- Do not use your outdoor hose except in emergencies.
- Do not waste water washing your car or cleaning outdoor areas of your home.
- Do not wash yourself by having a bath. Use your shower, if you have one, and wash only when necessary.

Heatwave

Although heatwaves are sometimes welcomed as part of good summer weather, they can also pose serious health challenges. Heatwaves in the UK have become more frequent while a heatwave in northern France in August 2003 resulted in approximately 15,000 deaths, particularly among the elderly due to heat-related conditions. Heatwaves can be exacerbated in urban areas where concrete and glass buildings retain the heat of the sun. Air quality is also reduced in urban areas. Heatwaves can exacerbate cardiovascular and respiratory diseases. Other effects of a heatwave are heat rash, heat exhaustion and heatstroke. (See first aid chapter for treatment of heatstroke.)

In order to decrease the risk of ill health at least or death at worst, it is important to be prepared for a heatwave. Sensible measures can reduce the risk of illness in a heatwave such as staying in cool, shady areas, keeping out of the sun during the hottest part of the day, wearing loose-fitting clothing, drinking cool drinks and sprinkling the body with cool water. Bowls of water and plants help to retain the moisture in the atmosphere. Leafy areas in parks, particularly near lakes, streams or rivers, are the best place to be as there is more cooling moisture in the atmosphere.

Effects of hot weather

Farm land and grassy areas can become cracked and dry in prolonged hot spells. Rail tracks can also become warped as the metal expands in high temeratures, leading to possible rail accidents.

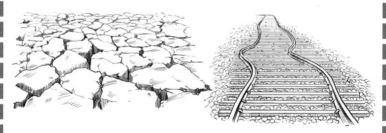

What to do in a heatwave

- Try to stay in the shade as much as possible.
- Put bowls full of water in your home and garden to try to keep some moisture in the atmopsphere.
- Wear lightweight, cotton clothing to keep your body cool.

Whatever your personal circumstances, it is wise to be prepared for the unexpected. Disasters happen when you least expect them. The better you can adapt quickly to fast-changing environments, the greater your chances of survival in a crisis. The more prepared you are physically and mentally, the better you will be able to endure extreme events or conditions.

For this reason, training for special forces soldiers often involves food deprivation and extremes of either heat or cold. They have to learn how to live off the land, to catch food and to build shelters.

Special forces soldiers are selected for their fitness and qualities of endurance, but perhaps more important than these elements is the determination and confidence that holds everything together, and which enables them to keep going when most people would have given up. Elite soldiers are often deployed into a crisis at short notice – insurgents, for example, do not tend to give advance warning when they seize hostages, and terrorists do not advertise where they might place their next bomb. Special forces,

. . . .

Left: No matter how fit you are, sleep and rest are essential for optimum performance in crisis situations.

2

A healthy mind and positive attitude is essential in preparing to survive a crisis.

Crisis Situations
Crisis
Survival
Psychology

Anger management

Learning how to manage anger is an important life skill and it is helpful in a crisis when a calm attitude can make a big difference in dealing with and overcoming emergencies.

therefore, need to be in a constant state of readiness so that when the call comes they can move at a moment's notice and adapt quickly to whatever circumstances they find themselves. They know that their lives and the lives of others depend on fast reactions and adaptability.

In a similar way, the average civilian also needs to be prepared both mentally and physically to deal with a crisis. The problem for the average civilian is that life, especially in urban environments, is normally relatively easy. Houses and places of work are often well heated and food is easily accessed, either by a short trip to a supermarket or by home delivery. The greatest stress the average shopper encounters is

Dealing with stress

If you can cope with stress, you will be in a better position to handle unexpected challenges such as a road rage incident.

TIP:
STRESS-MANAGEMENT BREATHING TECHNIQUE

- Either sit or stand in a relaxed position.
- Breathe in slowly through your nose up to a count of five.
- Exhale slowly through your mouth up to a count of eight.
- As you breathe, let your abdomen expand fully so that the breath goes down deep into your lungs.
- Repeat sequence, relaxing your body and mind as you do.

parking a car in a crowded car park or pushing a heavy trolley through crowded aisles. Of course, there are other stressors, such as traffic jams and crowded trains, and it is notable that there is often near panic when a train is cancelled. There is no denying that these things do cause real stress, and because we live sedentary lives, the effects of the stress on our bodies is magnified. There is little physical outlet for frustration when sitting in a traffic jam, for example.

Such frustrations are generally only temporary, and the extent of the frustration is normally in proportion to the extent that we are used to getting what we need quickly. Compare the difficulties encountered in travelling to the supermarket to buy fish for dinner with laying out fishing lines on a river to catch a fish that may be the only food you will have that day.

As suggested by the Latin phrase *mens sano in corpore sano* ('a healthy mind in a healthy body'), mental and physical preparedness

Preparation and determination

Preparation and a determined attitude are key to surviving a crisis situation. If you are prepared, with the right equipment, you will be better able to handle unexpected challenges in extreme circumstances.

are complementary. A fit, well-exercised body is likely to create a state of mental alertness. Stamina, 'the ability to sustain prolonged physical or mental effort' (Oxford Concise English Dictionary), is as essential for special forces soldiers as it is for anyone in a crisis. So is endurance. Another quality of special forces soldiers, as suggested by the SAS motto 'Who Dares Wins', is the determination to succeed. Special forces do not just participate – they win. When the chips are down, they survive. They come through. It is not just the physical fitness that gets them through, it is the mental determination that drives them.

WHERE TO START

People who have had military training have an advantage when faced with a crisis. Military forces personnel are invariably involved with the great outdoors. Soldiers are trained to be meticulous about their personal appearance and their equipment. Well-trained soldiers, even when they

Training and coping

Armed forces personnel increase their chances of survival through intensive training and correct preparation.

have become civilians, are likely to be instinctively aware of what they need for any kind of expedition, and have it to hand. When a crisis occurs, the 'training takes over'. This is a familiar phrase, but its importance cannot be overemphasized. There is little time to think in a crisis. If the scenario has been pre-rehearsed, however, an automatic response is possible. Self-discipline, training, teamwork and self-reliance are likely to help them to think more clearly and to take appropriate action.

For a civilian to emulate all this without military training is not easy, but the good news is that it is not impossible either. There are many civilian outdoor activities that mirror military physical training. Running, swimming, cycling and other sports will build up the levels of fitness that special forces soldiers require. Long-distance walking and climbing will produce the qualities of endurance so familiar to the special forces. Associated with such activities will be navigational and a host of other survival skills, including the ability to read the weather and cope in different climate zones.

Being involved in a variety of activities, such as those mentioned in the previous paragraph, will automatically enhance mental qualities such as determination, stamina and endurance. It will take tenacity and motivation, for example,

TIP:
STRESS-MANAGEMENT PROGRESSIVE MUSCLE RELAXATION

- Find somewhere quiet where you can relax for a few minutes.
- Either sit or lie down.
- Tense up all the muscles in your face as you inhale for a count of eight, then relax them as you breathe out.
- Tense up your neck and shoulders and inhale to a count of eight. As you exhale, make sure all the muscles relax as you do so.
- Tense the muscles around your chest and stomach while you inhale to a count of eight. Relax them as you exhale.
- Tense the muscles in your buttocks, thighs, calves and feet while you inhale to a count of eight. Relax them as you exhale.

Fatigue

Lack of water and sleep can quickly cause mental fatigue. Always ensure you have enough provisions for any journeys.

to put together a running fitness programme, for example, and to stick to it even when the weather is cold or you are tired from work in the office.

MENTAL PREPARATION

A crisis or a disaster will cause stress and often panic. This mental state is not conducive to rational thinking and rational action. Special forces soldiers usually start off with one major advantage: they willingly go into a crisis scenario having prepared themselves in detail to deal with both the expected (for example, terrorists who will shoot at them) and the unexpected (for example, panicking

hostages who get in the way). They try to cover every eventuality so that they know exactly what to do when the occasion arises.

In a safe civilian world, we do not normally expect a crisis to occur, so our motivation to prepare is reduced. Our newspapers, however, are filled every day with news of emergencies that happen to normal people, including fires and flooding. It makes sense, therefore, for us to prepare for these eventualities. If you are travelling abroad – for example, to a politically unstable part of the world – or if you are heading off on an expedition into

Knowing the ground

Effective use of a map can be of critical importance in a crisis, as it will help you to find the quickest route to safety.

the wilderness, the motive for preparation or emergency conditioning is all the greater.

Special forces soldiers have areas in which they specialize, but they also train across a wide range of disciplines, including mountaineering, diving, abseiling and parachuting. This gives them a particularly wide range of skills and prepares them to cope with an equally wide range of challenges. In a similar way, the more you prepare yourself to meet different eventualities, the better able you will be to deal with them effectively when they arise.

Fire drill

Depending on what you think is likely to happen, which in turn depends on where you are and what you are planning to do, it is a good idea to do the equivalent of a fire drill for each of these eventualities. In a classic fire drill, institutions such as schools set off the fire alarms so that pupils and teachers learn where the exits and meeting points are in a real emergency. Air crew run through drills before every flight. You can physically walk through your own drills, along with any associates, so that everyone knows precisely where to go and what to do in emergency.

You can also prepare yourself by visualizing the emergency scenario and thinking through your actions, along with a successful outcome.

TIP:
POSITIVE VISUALIZATION

Studies have shown that mentally visualizing (imagining) certain situations, and how you would act in them, can contribute to a successful outcome in the real world. This is the mental equivalent of a rehearsal.

You can add some realism by mimicking the physical motions, as if you were acting in reality. For example, if you are planning to ski or snowboard in an area that you know to be dangerous, you can imagine the action you would take if an avalanche began to develop. Imagine heading at the correct angle towards the edge of the moving slab of snow,

maintaining the momentum and entering into an area of stable snow. Or imagine what you would do if you were caught up in an avalanche: how you would let go of your backpack and of any other heavy equipment; imagine deploying any safety equipment, such as an airbag; and carrying out the approved 'backstroke' swimming motions to stay as close to the surface as possible.

For example, if you are entering a ski competition, you can put your ski boots on and stand in your room, then imagine going down the hill, making similar movements with your

This means that you will have effectively pre-recorded an action plan that you can draw on in an emergency when there is little time to think.

PHYSICAL EFFECTS

Special forces and general military training is designed to test the reactions and behaviour of individuals when usual life-support mechanisms

arms and legs as you go on your imaginary journey downhill. Imagine dealing successfully with all the difficult turns, jumps and obstacles. Imagine crossing the finishing line in front of a cheering crowd. You can use similar techniques to imagine what you would do in an emergency, such as getting off a capsizing boat or ship.

are removed, such as food, warmth and rest. It is one thing to test somebody's physical performance when they are well fed and have adequate water and sleep, it is

TIP:
UK HEALTH AND SAFETY EXECUTIVE GUIDELINES FOR RISK ASSESSMENT

- Identify the hazards and associated risks.
- Identify who is potentially at risk and how.
- Identify the precautions or control measures to minimize the risk, including any further action required to reduce the risk to an acceptable level.
- Record your findings.
- Review the risk assessment periodically.

another to do so when these supports are not available.

Lack of water alone can have a variety of side effects, one of which is a deterioration in brain function. To think and make urgent decisions becomes much more difficult under such conditions. Lack of water can lead to serious dehydration and eventually death. A number one survival priority, therefore, is to preserve available water, set out a workable regime for water use and

Family outing

Even a family hike can turn into a crisis if the weather changes unexpectedly, someone gets injured or the party gets lost. Good preparation and equipment will help you overcome the challenge.

find sources of water if the existing supply is limited. It is best to make these decisions before your brain function is reduced.

Cold will have a debilitating effect on the body and reduce the will to take action. Cold can be overcome temporarily by physical activity. Military training often involves exposing recruits to extreme cold, such as swimming in a river or lake at night, in order to gauge the reactions of the recruits afterwards. Apart from physical activity, cold can be mitigated by teamwork. For example, a team can keep each other awake in extreme cold before they are rescued or while they have time to reach safety.

Obviously the adverse effects of cold can be mitigated by proper clothing. Special forces soldiers soon learn to use clothing carefully. When they are working up a sweat through long walks with heavy loads, they will keep any warm clothing in their rucksacks and, if it is cold, they will put on the warm clothing when they stop. This technique prevents the warm clothing from becoming soaked with sweat and losing its warming properties. Special forces soldiers, like many active outdoor people, are aware of layering principles, which means that warm air is held between layers of clothing that can be added or removed as necessary according to the conditions or level of activity. Such layering systems can include

technical clothing which, while being extremely light, has a very high warmth factor. If you carry such equipment with you, you will be more confident in a crisis and vastly improve your ability to cope.

DO YOUR HOMEWORK

An important part of mental preparation is knowing that you have done your homework, that you have a sound knowledge of the region you are visiting and that you are prepared for any eventuality. Many of the most attractive places to visit in the world are in areas of political instability, or at least areas where the liberal political and legal freedoms that are sometimes taken for granted in the Western world do not exist.

Before leaving, make sure that you inform yourself on both the political and cultural background of the country or region you are visiting as well as the current political situation and any likely developments. Access to such information can be obtained in a number of ways, including government information portals and reputable economic, geopolitical and current affairs websites and magazines. Much of this information can be obtained free of charge.

Read as much as you can about local customs and how best to deal with people in the areas you will visit. Aspects of behaviour that are considered normal in the West may be seen as offensive in other

Dehydration

Dehydration has a crippling effect on the mind and body. Effective management of the water supply is key for survival. Finding or collecting clean water is also an essential skill.

countries. This may cover a range of situations, from how to negotiate with local taxi drivers to what women should wear. If the people in the country or region you are visiting find that you are sympathetic towards their culture and way of behaving, you are likely to find that your visit

TIP:
ROYAL GEOGRAPHICAL SOCIETY RISK ASSESSMENT

Here is an assessment guide to potential risks based on one provided by the Royal Geographical Society (RGS) Expedition Handbook. The RGS recommend that you go through all the 'what if' scenarios so that you are: a) prepared and know what to do if something goes wrong; and b) have the necessary equipment and supplies. What follows is a list of the dangers and situations to evaluate in any expedition or adventure.

The Team
- Health and fitness (including previous medical conditions) – increased risk of existing health problems on expedition, leading to serious illness / death
- Attitude and behaviour – increased risk of ignoring control measures, resulting in illness / injury
- Experience and training – reduces risk

Personal equipment
- Serious injury / illness resulting from inadequate equipment / equipment failure

The Environment
- Mountains / sea / desert / jungle
- Altitude sickness / drowning / heat problems
- Climate and weather conditions
- Heat- and cold-related injury / death

will run much more smoothly. More importantly, you will also have a much better chance of negotiating your way out of difficult situations.

Environment

You will also need to thoroughly acquaint yourself with the environmental conditions of the

- Wildlife (including insects) – attack / poisoning through bites / stings / disease

Health
- Endemic disease (e.g. dengue fever / Japanese encephalitis)
- Malaria
- AIDS / HIV
- Polluted water
- Contaminated food
- Hygiene / living conditions

Local Population
- Political instability / coup / kidnapping / imprisonment
- Attitudes to foreigners / cultural differences
- Attack / rape / theft / mugging

Expedition Activity
- Trekking / climbing / mountaineering
- Altitude sickness / falls from height

River crossing
- Water-based activities (caving / cave diving)
- Equipment failure / inappropriate use
- Games / sports activities
Injury / incapacitation

Travel and camp life
- Transport (public / private)
- Road / water conditions
- Camp hazards (stoves / fires / flooding / avalanche / wildlife)
- Accommodation / hotels
- Fire / electrocution

TIP: TRAVEL CHECKLIST

- Passport with at least six months before expiry
- Visas and any other documentation required for the country you are visiting
- Health insurance
- Travel insurance
- Vaccinations for local infections and diseases
- Visit your GP before you go
- Copy essential documents
- Leave emergency contact details
- Local money / travellers' cheques
- Valid driving licence (international)
- Identify your local national consulate

region you will be visiting, taking into account that many environmental conditions will be unpredictable. Take note of the most recent meteorological forecasts, including long-term forecasts for the region. Are there any hurricane warnings? Have there been any reports of forest fires? What are the snow conditions?

Environmental conditions such as these are covered in more detail in later chapters.

Medical

Especially if you are travelling from Europe to a region such as Africa or Southeast Asia, you will almost certainly need to update yourself on the vaccinations required for the region, such as malaria or cholera. Cholera is endemic in areas of Africa, the Middle East and South America and has a mortality rate of up to 50 per cent if not effectively treated. Infections such as cholera will also be influenced by the local political and environmental situation. You need to find out whether there have been recent earthquakes or political unrest in the region you have visited, to check whether it may have affected the water supply.

Apart from vaccinations against such infections and diseases, you should also be aware of sensible sanitary precautions, which include actions as basic as careful handwashing and the cleaning of eating utensils.

Paperwork

You cannot take anything for granted when travelling abroad and you may need a range of extra documentation, including visas, before you enter a country. You also need to check such basic facts as whether your passport is due for renewal. It may be valid on

RISK ASSESSMENT MNEMONIC – CRISIS

C – Clarify the hazards and risks.

R – Reassess and revise where necessary.

I – Involve all participants in the process.

S – State it simply in writing.

I – If it's too risky, don't do it.

S – Share knowledge and experience.

the day of travel, for example, but will it expire while you are away? In some countries, you may be arrested and held in detention if your documents are not in order. It is also a good idea to make copies of essential documentation and to keep them in a safe place in case you are robbed or are involved in an emergency where you lose your documents. Keep spare physical copies as well as storing them in a safe area online.

MEDITATION TECHNIQUES

Meditation techniques can be useful for calming the mind when it is under stress, or preparing the mind for stresses to come. The following is a typical meditation routine.

- Choose a time of day when you are least likely to be disturbed. The evening may be a good time, after the rush and activity of the day.
- Find a quiet place where you can be alone and isolated from distracting noises and interruptions.
- Sit somewhere comfortable in an upright position. The idea is to meditate, not to doze off.
- Allow your body and mind to relax, while remaining focused.
- It is likely that your mind will be still running through the day's issues. Try not to follow up any particular thought – just let them drop one by one.
- Try to breathe steadily. A technique for regulating your breathing sometimes used by runners in training is to take three long and deep breaths through the mouth, exhaling each one slowly through the nose. This brings your breathing under control and helps to calm you.
- It can be helpful to focus on a particular word or image to stop

the mind pursuing vain thoughts. Such a word, or 'mantra' (to use the term from Indian religions), might be 'peace' or 'calm', which reminds you what you are trying to achieve for both your body and mind.

- The mantra is not necessarily the focus of your thoughts – the point of it is to bring them back to the centre when they are distracted. If you are able, try to keep your mind free from any thoughts for as long as possible. Even though you will be unaware of it, this will help to strengthen the muscles of the mind.

The regular practice of emptying the mind in meditation creates a clear space for productive thoughts and helps you to set a right order of priorities. You can then formulate clearer plans, just as it is easier to make plans on a clear desk than on a cluttered one (unless, of course, you thrive on chaos!).

Although meditation is largely associated with religious practice, the benefits apply to all. In a crisis, clear actions are imperative. You may have to decide, for example, whether to build a shelter and wait for rescue or to take what you can and walk to a safer area. You will

Clear mind

Practising meditation techniques can help to keep the mind clear in a stressful situation where there is a tendency to be confused by the pressure of circumstances.

TIP:
DOING NOTHING IN A CRISIS

Strangely enough, one of the best ways of ensuring effective action in a crisis is by doing nothing. This does not mean, of course, doing nothing when urgent action is required in an emergency. It means taking the time to prepare the mind and bring it into focus regularly whenever there is an opportunity to do so.

The discipline of stopping the headlong run of activity will sharpen the mind, generate a stronger sense of purpose, provide more focus and make it more likely that you will act in an appropriate way when there is little time for thought. If you have trained your mind to step off the treadmill on regular occasions, it is more likely that you will have calm and effective thoughts in a crisis.

need a plan and a timetable for the day, taking into account changing circumstances. Having a clear mind, strengthened by meditation and focus, you are better able to plan an appropriate response. As you may be affected by cold, heat or a lack of water and/or food, and as these may affect your moods, inclinations and strength, a clearly thought-out plan will help you to set priorities and to stick to them, and to make decisions that are more likely to ensure your survival.

CONFIDENCE

Using meditation techniques and discipline, you can think more clearly and set out a plan of action. Another ingredient you will need is the faith that your plans and decisions and actions will have a successful outcome. This quality requires both faith in your own judgement and abilities as well as faith that events will turn out for the best.

The Oxford English Dictionary definition of 'confidence' is 'the belief that one can have faith or rely on someone or something; a positive feeling arising from an appreciation of one's own abilities; self-assurance'. Of course, the circumstances in which you demonstrate confidence most fully are those which are least likely to lead to such feelings. In a potentially life-threatening situation, it takes confidence to envisage a successful outcome against all the odds.

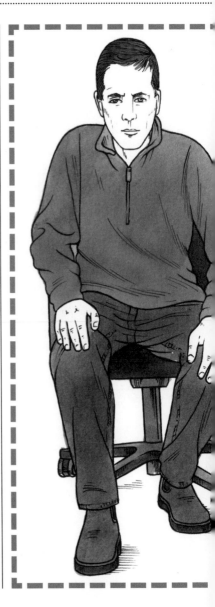

Self-assurance

Self assurance and confidence often show in a person's attitude and posture. Confidence can be built up by facing and overcoming challenges. It is enhanced by the will to survive in difficult situations.

The advantage of a spirit of confidence is that it tends to feed off itself and produce its own success story. Someone who acts confidently sets off a chain of positive reactions that are likely to throw the odds in his favour. He is likely to get a positive reaction from other people and to inspire them to do their best. He is more likely to go the extra mile, which may enable him to reach safety.

Confidence is a difficult notion to pin down, just as it is difficult to say why one person is confident and another is not. A confident person may be someone whose experiences have given him self-assurance and self-worth, despite his failings and ups and downs, and a belief that things will generally turn out for the best in the end. Confident people are those who can accept themselves as they are and can cope when circumstances are unfamiliar or when people behave differently. Someone with a less-secure background may be less confident, but this is not always the case. Sometimes tough circumstances, create a tough, coping attitude, which in turn breeds confidence.

You may be confident because you have had a strong, nurturing background or because you have had to learn to cope. You may be unconfident because you have had an over-protected background where you did not have to learn to cope,

make decisions and stand on your own two feet. Whatever the circumstances, every person will differ in their level of confidence and because it is so difficult to pin down, it may be helpful to try to describe what is most likely to produce confidence.

Confidence can be generated by having the courage to face up to difficult challenges and to overcome them. Theodore Roosevelt said that he gradually acquired confidence by confronting those things of which he was afraid: 'There were all kinds of things of which I was afraid at first, ranging from grizzly bears to mean horses and gun fighters, but by acting as if I was not afraid I gradually ceased to be afraid.'

The difference between a confident and unconfident person may lie in the readiness to accept risks and failure. Even if someone takes a risk and fails, he has at least had a go and has learned something from it. Another person may say they knew something would fail and therefore it was not worth trying anyway. They will never, however, have the real experience to build on.

SELF-ACCEPTANCE

Another source of confidence is being yourself and accepting yourself. If you try to conform to the expectations of others the whole time, you will be like a puppet on a string. You will be liable to be manipulated by others as they try to impose on you their own image of how you should be in order to suit themselves. A confident person does not depend upon the opinion of others.

A confident person is essentially independent minded. Although he may listen to the opinion of others, ultimately he will make his own decisions about how to live his life. A confident person is also likely to remain calm when faced with a crisis. His calmness will help him to make sound decisions and to take appropriate action. He is less likely to allow himself to be hurried into making mistakes, especially in stressful situations.

TIP:
COUNTERING NEGATIVE CRITICISM

In a crisis, you are likely to be faced with negative reactions from other people. This may involve questioning your leadership or your decisions. You may have little support for any plans that you make. In view of this, you need to prepare yourself mentally to deal with any eventuality and to have the courage to carry through decisions once you have made a thorough assessment of the challenge. When facing criticism from others, you have to accept yourself and remind yourself that you are taking action that you believe to be the best in the circumstances. Stress can often be caused by other people's negative behaviour or refusal to acknowledge our efforts or achievements. Often we use up a lot of time and energy trying to make people approve of us and we make our happiness dependent on their approval. When faced with negative (as opposed to constructive) criticism, learn to accept yourself. An Italian philosopher, Romano Guardini, once wrote: 'The act of self-acceptance is the root of all things. I must agree to be the person who I am. Agree to have the qualifications which I have. Agree to live within the limitations set for me... The clarity and the courageousness of this acceptance is the foundation of all existence.'

STRESS MANAGEMENT

The underlying theme that runs through this book is preparation. Confidence is bred from preparation, either because someone has experienced similar difficulties and obstacles before and learned to overcome them or because she has prepared herself to meet those challenges and to cope with them.

A crisis is an unexpected situation of an extreme nature. It is more than likely going to create stress of varying degrees, depending on its nature and severity and on the level of experience of those involved. It follows, therefore, that having a well-rehearsed backup plan is an excellent way of minimizing stress. The time when the crisis occurs is not the time to work out a backup plan. The sooner a problem is dealt with, the less likely it will be that it will get out of control.

Another excellent way of combating stress is to be physically

Fire in the kitchen

In a crisis situation, the worst thing you can do is panic. For example, when faced with a kitchen pan fire, quick effective action based on correct preparation will avert further damage.

Stress in the field

A crisis can be overwhelming; however, once you have considered your options and established the way forward, decisive action is the key to survival.

TIP:
STRESS EFFECTS

- The body releases chemicals such as cortisol.
- If these chemicals are not used through physical activity – fight or flight – they remain in the body and put undue pressure on the heart and other systems.
- A stressed person will be irritable and liable to react negatively to others.
- Stress makes it more difficult to sleep and the sufferer feels tired.
- Concentration becomes more difficult under stress, as does the ability to make decisions.
- A stressed person may suffer from indigestion and other unpleasant side effects.
- A stressed person may feel depressed and anxious.
- If you are stressed, you will be less inclined to take appropriate action.

fit. A stressful situation will have a number of unpleasant side effects, including increased heart rate and blood pressure and a sense of confusion. If you are fit, your heart rate will not go up so high and so you will remain more in control. You are more likely to remain focused and to make appropriate decisions.

Although stress is to some extent a part and parcel of daily life, and can be part of a positive life programme in which we meet challenges and overcome them, overwhelming stress erodes our ability to cope in a crisis

What might be stressful for one person might not be for another. Stress is directly connected to our perception of how well we can cope in a given situation. A rock-climbing expert, for example, might be unnerved by a dismasted yacht, but well able to cope with an emergency on a cliff face.

To cope with stress, the body and mind need time out if they are to perform. Some people need more sleep than others, and if you do not have adequate sleep you may end up with a sleep deficit. All this will add to stress. In a crisis, opportunities for sleep may be limited, but you still need to be aware that your mind and body will need rest so that you can recuperate and plan. Try to make plans when you are most alert, and set reasonable goals for the day. If you set reasonable goals and achieve them, you should experience a sense of accomplishment and you will feel more confident. Another way to defeat stress is to list all the factors that are causing the stress and to deal with them one by one.

Managing stress

Military personnel receive training in managing the stress of capture and interrogation. A tough mental attitude helps to combat stress.

DECISION-MAKING AND ACTION

If stress is largely caused by a sense of not being able to cope with problems that appear to be insurmountable, or which are so numerous that we cannot decide where to begin tackling them, it follows that any decisions and actions we take to deal with the problems will help to reduce stress and move us closer to our goals. Again, we need to remember that personalities differ. Some people are more active than others, some are more decisive than others, some think profoundly about things, some are good at thinking on their feet. In a crisis situation, however, decisive action needs to be taken one way or another so that you do not become overwhelmed by the magnitude of the problems and challenges.

Evaluation

First, evaluate all your options, taking into account various factors such as climate, geography, the number of people involved, their state of health, their abilities and also

Taking action

TIP:
PARETO ANALYSIS

The Pareto Principle is that some 80 per cent of effects in any situation come from 20 per cent of the causes. This principle was originally applied in economics, but for survival it means that if you can identify the key problems (20 per cent of the total) you can solve the rest of the problems (80 per cent) without having to address them directly. Score each problem on a seriousness scale of 1–10. Once this is done, you will have a much better idea of what the really significant challenges are and which issues are less important.

Quick and effective action can save lives. If you know what to do, you will be much more effective in a crisis situation.

available equipment or shelter. One way of evaluating the problems is by working out how serious each challenge is on a scale of 1–10. If, for example, lack of food or water is towards 10 on the scale, it will obviously be a top priority to find them. If food and water are less of a problem and geographical obstacles are a major problem, you may want to focus on making the best out of your current position and finding ways of signalling for help. Whatever the circumstances, an intelligent analysis of the problems is likely to lead to the best decisions and courses of action.

Assess and share

In order to promote decision-making and action, look upon each problem as a challenge that can be overcome. Remember, even if you cannot go straight over an obstacle, there are

TIP:
SIX THINKING HATS

This decision-making tool was developed by the logic expert Edward de Bono. The tool aims to extend the possibilities of problem solving by looking at problems from different perspectives. In each case, you have to imagine that you put on a particular hat, and that each hat relates to a specific mode of thinking.

White hat
- With this hat on, you look coldly and analytically at the available data, or in a crisis you may want to summarize and take stock of your situation, your supplies and so on.

Red hat
- With this hat on, you look at your position from an intuitive and emotional perspective, taking into account your own and others' gut reactions.

Black hat
- Look at your current situation and available options from a pessimistic standpoint. Look at the worse-case scenarios and what might go wrong if you embark on a particular course of action. Thinking with this hat should help you to be realistic about problems. For example, you may plan

sometimes ways round it. One problem might also be diminished to insignificance by action taken to address another problem.

Before making decisions, it may be a good procedure to invite any ideas from others who are present. A problem that looms large in your mind might be less of a problem for someone else, who may have particular experience in dealing with the issue.

By taking action to list problems, they become compartmentalized and to some extent externalized. They no a long walk to safety, but you admit with your black hat on that two members of your group are not fit enough to do the distance. How will you get round that problem? With the black hat on you may hope for the best, but prepare for the worst.

Yellow hat

- This is the sunny hat. With this hat on, you look at all the positive sides of your situation and courses of action. For example, you may be stranded but you have enough food and water to last you a few days. How will you take advantage of that situation? In a crisis, looking at the positive side will be a morale booster for yourself and for others

Green hat

- This is the creative hat that allows plenty of scope for free thought and ideas. Sometimes this kind of thinking throws up possibilities that can be turned into practical reality.

Blue hat

- This hat represents the chair of the meeting, who may want to analyze the practical responsibilities in an otherwise wild idea or ask for more creative thinking if the ideas are too hidebound, cautious or pessimistic. For example, there is a river between you and safety. Going the long way round will mean a lengthy detour and you may not have enough supplies, or team members may be unfit or injured.

longer have the same power to wash around in your mind, causing stress and worry. Short, crisp descriptions of the issues on paper will help to keep them all manageable. Once you start to evaluate the challenges and begin to make decisions based on their scale of importance, your mind is likely to carry on dealing with the issues even when you have other things to do or are resting. You may find that when you return to your list, you come up with other creative ideas for ways of dealing with it.

Emergency priority list

- Difficult terrain—no easy route out

- Team member with fractured ankle

- Team member with concussion

- Food OK—3 days' supply

- Water OK—3 days

- Medical equipment OK

- Radio works

Conclusion/action:
1. Treat casualties
2. Make shelter
3. Rest
4. Radio for help

Recharging your batteries

Never underestimate the importance of sleep. Adequate time for sleep should be built into any survival plan.

REST AND SLEEP

As has been mentioned above, sleep is essential for the body to regain its strength for future challenges and to maintain mental and physical effort. Yet sleep is not simply a case of taking time out. Scientists have shown that during the period of sleep, and especially during 'Rapid Eye Movement' (REM) sleep, the brain is at work, providing creative solutions to problems. Hence the expression 'sleep on it'.

Ideally, you should sleep for between seven and nine hours per night. This can be supplemented with 'napping' for about 30 minutes between 2pm and 5pm in the afternoon. Napping at other times

may adversely affect your sleep patterns and concentration. A crisis is obviously not conducive to a good night's sleep but, on the other hand, you need to be aware that rest and sleep are part of your survival programme. Your decision-making and planning need to take account of the need for sleep and this may include, for example, constructing adequate shelters so that you and your group can rest. If you are in a desert environment, for example, you may want to sleep during the day so that you can walk during the cool hours of the night. Whatever your circumstances, you must recognize that without sleep your mental and physical powers will be degraded.

A ccidents and emergencies can take on a number of forms, from social breakdown following political unrest through the after-effects of natural disasters to the ongoing threat of terrorism. Emergencies can also occur in the home or while travelling. Although sometimes these threats can be heightened when travelling to other countries, often they are close to home – whether it be snowstorms in the United States or floods in Britain. In each case, careful forward planning and mental toughness will help you to cope. This chapter aims to help you to be aware and be prepared.

SOCIAL BREAKDOWN

It is possible for either a temporary or longer-term collapse of the social order to take place. This may be the result of a revolution or it may follow a major natural or man-made disaster such as earthquakes or military attack. The result may be population displacement and the collapse of all or most public services and utilities, ranging from lack of police control to lack of gas or water.

Major centres of social unrest include parts of Africa, the Middle

. . . .

Left: Whether in the home, on the street, or on public transport, be prepared for an emergency.

Accidents and emergencies can happen where you least expect them to.

Crisis Stuations

Accidents and Emergencies

When law and order breaks down

A whole new range of dangers can develop following a natural disaster, including looting and animals running wild.

East, South America, parts of Asia and Eastern Europe. In some areas, local warlords have taken over control from central government authorities. Cities in the develpped world have also suffered a breakdown of social order, especially following natural disasters, such as floods and earthquakes.

What to do

If you live in or are visiting a politically unstable area, make sure you are prepared with essential supplies in case basic utilities and shopping outlets no longer function. Depending on your circumstances, this could mean storing enough for several months. This will include food that will not perish and plenty of drinking water. You will also need fuel for portable gas stoves or wood or coal-burning fires. A supply of warm clothing will also be necessary (if you are in a cold region) as well as blankets, sleeping bags and so on.

It is important to have a working radio to keep up to date with the political situation and to help you to decide whether to move out of the area or stay until the situation improves. You may need to consider alternative sanitation, depending on the amount of available water for flushing and whether there is still a supply of water to the premises. Use old water, such as washing water, for flushing.

Create networks with trusted people but do not become involved with people you do not know who may wish to influence you for their own political ends. In an unpoliced social situation, many people may be taking things that do not belong to them and may become aggressive. Be circumspect about obtaining what you need for survival without becoming involved in confrontations.

The lack of any normal social parameters will create stress. Make sure that you remain calm and on top of the situation. Allow a safety-valve for stress by creating some form of recreation. There will need to be some form of leadership and agreement about what roles different people should have. Once individuals have a role that fits with their skills and talent, they should feel happier and more motivated. The systems your create in you small community should be a microcosm of typical systems of order and fairness in a typical free, organized society.

EPIDEMICS

An epidemic means the widespread occurrence of a particular disease and it partly depends on the number of people in a particular population who are susceptible to the disease. As immunity increases, the epidemic decreases and then disappears. Great epidemics in world history include smallpox, influenza, malaria, bubonic plague (the 'Black Death'), tuberculosis, cholera, AIDS, yellow fever, typhus, polio and swine flu.

To prepare for an epidemic, keep informed on the status of any disease and be prepared for a

Face masks

Medical authorities recommend wearing face masks as a way of limiting contamination from viruses, such as H1Ni and bird flu. The mask should be made from micro-pores, which filter air for respiration, stopping micro-organisms from penetrating through. Doctors use something similar during surgeries.

period of quarantine. Gather emergency supplies just as you would for any other natural or man-made disaster, to include water, food, medical equipment and so on. Inform your family and associates of what they should do in an emergency. Find out about sheltering yourself in the home from possible contaminants. You may want to identify a room in your home, preferably with an adjoining bathroom, where the family can shelter for the duration. Quarantine may be necessary for people who have been exposed to a dangerous disease. Keep in touch with official health bodies about quarantine arrangements.

During an epidemic or pandemic, there is likely to be a range of advice offered by authorities, which

will include vaccination and other medical treatment as well as advice on travel. Make sure you keep up to date with the latest advice, either through the media or world wide web or by phoning relevant bodies. It is important to develop a positive and resilient mental attitude so that you can cope with an epidemic, as with any other disaster.

LOSS OF POWER SUPPLY

The power supply to your office or home may be interrupted for a number of reasons, including natural disasters or adverse weather conditions, sabotage and terrorism or social breakdown.

Whatever the reason, if any of these events are likely to occur, ensure that you have enough fuel as well as other sources of energy such as batteries, wood or coal. If the gas supply is interrupted, make sure you turn it off in case the supply is restored and gas starts leaking into your home.

Check that there are no broken pipes nearby or any downed electricity cables and warn members of your group not to touch any cables. Take care when attending to any electrical fittings in the house that the electricity is turned off in case the supply is restored while you are still working on it.

Keeping warm

In the event of losing your power supply, stay in one room, huddle together, and use all available materials to keep warm – blankets, curtains, towels and newspapers.

TERRORISM

At the time of writing, the US Department of Homeland Security National Threat Advisory was 'Elevated', while the threat level in the US airline sector was 'High' or 'Orange.' The assessment by the British Security Service (MI5) of the terrorist threat to the United Kingdom was 'substantial': this rating meant that a terrorist attack was a strong possibility.

From the Western perspective, the greatest threat is from international terrorist groups such as al-Qaida and its associated networks. The attack on the New York World Trade Center twin towers on 11 September 2001 was the work of al-Qaida, as was the attack on the Madrid railway system

Suspicious packages

Be aware of someone placing a package with undue care in a litter bin. It may be an explosive device.

WORLD TERRORISM

On September 11, 2001 the United States suffered the worst terrorist atrocity in history, as nearly 3000 people were killed when four airliners were turned into flying bombs to attack the World Trade Center and the Pentagon. Despite this horrific event, the United States actually stands as one of the world's safest places in terms of terrorism, at least in crude numbers of incidents. Terrorist attacks in Israel, for instance, have occurred at a rate of one or two a week, with enormous impact on the social and cultural life of the nation.

Overall, the worldwide occurrence of terrorism is declining since it peaked in the 1970s and 1980s. In 1986, there were 897 terrorist attacks globally, falling to 666 in 1987, 427 in 1993, and 321 terrorist attacks in 1994. (Data: US State Department) However, casualty figures from the individual attacks have risen. In the 1970s, property bombings accounted for 70 per cent of terrorist assaults and direct targeting of people 30 per cent. Today the reverse is true, as terrorists seek to capitalize on public fear and horror.

on 11 March 2004 and the series of bombings on the London Underground system on 7 July 2005.

As al-Qaida is a highly diffused terrorist organization (it has even been called an 'idea' rather than an organization), with many cells and sympathisers, the threat has been difficult to monitor. British immigrant nationals, for example, with no loyalty to the British state were known to operate abroad and to undertake terrorist training in camps in Afghanistan and Pakistan. The terrorist threat in the United Kingdom has escalated, with about 2000 terrorist suspects in the UK at the time of writing, covering some 200 networks, and with at least 30 active terrorist plots under investigation by the security services. In 2001 there were only 250 terrorist suspects under investigation in the UK. Attacks on US and UK interests abroad has also been an ongoing issue. This includes attacks on consulates and embassies, on military and naval assets and on individuals. As far as ordinary citizens are concerned, terrorist attacks are highly random and totally unexpected. Motivated by their particular ideology, terrorists have no care whatsoever for the safety of innocent individuals and often have little desire to justify their cause. Their behaviour is characterized by total ruthlessness and their only concern is how much damage they can do to the state or states that they oppose. There is, therefore, no recourse to international law when dealing with terrorists.

Although warnings are sometimes given by members of terrorist groups before a bomb attack, on the whole the terrorist uses the slaughter of innocent civilians as a means of attracting attention. As terrorists often use bombs to attack transport facilities or buildings, you should follow advice in earlier chapters of this book covering preparation, awareness, fire hazards and so on.

Bombs

If a bomb goes off in a building.

- Do not attempt to use the lifts/elevators.
- Stay close to walls.
- Keep clear of windows, especially if they are cracked or shattered, unless you need to signal for help.

- Do not use matches or lighters in case there is a gas leak and you set off a secondary explosion.
- Do not touch or pick up any loose electrical wires or cables.
- If you are trapped, try knocking on a pipe or radiator to attract the attention of rescuers.
- If the bomb goes off outside your building:
- Do not go outside.
- Do not stay close to windows in case there is a second explosion that shatters the glass.

Chemical, biological or radiological (CBR) attack

Emergency services such as fire fighters are trained and equipped to provide on-the-scene decontamination of large numbers of people following a CBR attack. Health services are also trained to provide relevant treatment. The best way of coping with these incidents is to remain in the locality prior to decontamination. Expert advice on CBR incidents can be provided by emergency services, police and where relevant military forces.

- If you are outside, keep upwind of the area of the incident.
- If you have any form of protective equipment, such as a face, mask, you should put this on. If you have a gas mask, blow through it to vent any contaminants that may have got into the mask.

- If you do not have specialist protective equipment, you should cover all exposed areas of your skin with clothing, including hats and gloves for hands and head and scarves for the face.
- If there is contaminant inside a building you are in, evacuate the building as far as possible from the source of the contaminant. Keep windows and doors closed behind you.
- If you are outside and the contaminant is outside, get into a building and seal all entrances, including doors and windows and turn off any air conditioning systems. You can seal gaps around doors and windows with tape or with other materials.

Preventative measures

The best way to deal with terrorists is to identify and deter them before they have a chance to act. If you notice suspicious behaviour by an individual or group of individuals, report it to the police. For example, someone may visit a particular location at unusual times. He may hang around or try to conceal himself. He may be unusually serious and not wish to communicate with anyone. If you think an incident is imminent, call the police via the emergency telephone line.

If there has recently been an attack, particularly an attack on the transport system, stay clear of public transport until the threat has reduced.

TIP: OFFICIAL UK GOVERNMENT ADVICE ON CBR ATTACKS

- Move away from the immediate source of danger.

- But wait for the emergency services to arrive and examine you and, if necessary, decontaminate you.

- If you go home untreated, you could contaminate others and make the incident worse.

Furthermore, in the wake of an incident or a major threat, do not behave suspiciously yourself. The security services will be in a high state of alert and looking for other potential bombers. They may need to carry out routine checks on individuals. Remain calm and do exactly what they say and do not attempt to evade them.

Suspicious activity

If you see someone leave a package or a suitcase anywhere and the walk away, you should warn an official or the police.

You can try telling the individual they have forgotten something to see how they react. If someone is placing a bomb in a receptacle such as a waste-paper bin, they may do so with unusual care in case it goes off. Keep clear of the area and warn the emergency services. Take note of which direction the suspect went afterwards.

Car bombs

Cars have always been a popular way for terrorists to plant bomb devices. Car bombs can be activated in a number of ways, including opening the vehicle's doors, starting the engine, or depressing the accelerator or brake pedals.

Terrorists may pose as workmen doing a job on a building. If their van is unmarked and there are suspicious types of activity, check with someone that the work has been approved.

Terrorist attacks – means of delivery

Terrorists have a number of options for delivering bombs to a particular location. The problem for the public and the security services is that terrorists are ordinary citizens and mostly use normal forms of transport and act in a conventional way.

Vehicle bombs

Vehicle bombs are an effective means for delivering explosives, as the terrorist can create a larger bomb with a correspondingly larger impact. A car, van or lorry can carry a bomb weighing several tonnes. To help counter vehicle bombs, report to the police any suspicious vehicles near your home or place of work, including vehicles you do not recognize or which have been apparently abandoned.

Personal explosives

These are bombs carried to their locations by individuals. The bomb may be strapped to the terrorist's body, hidden under clothing, or it may be carried in a rucksack or a briefcase.

A portable bomb of this kind may weigh up to 25kg (55lb), though a

TIP: SUSPICIOUS VEHICLES

The following signs could alert you to a potential car bomb.

- A vehicle that is parked illegally, near a significant building or possible target
- A vehicle that has apparently been abandoned
- A vehicle that has been parked along the route or place of a special event, such as a parade
- A vehicle obviously weighted down on its suspension at the rear; this may indicate that the boot (trunk) contains a heavy explosive device.
- The first action when dealing with a genuinely suspicious vehicle is to contact the police. Warn others away and wait until the police arrive.

rucksack bomb will probably weigh about 12kg (26kg). The bomb may be packed with shrapnel such as nails and other metal objects to increase the anti-personnel effect.

109

Suicide bombers

Someone nervously handling a backpack in a public place with undue care may be carrying an explosive device.

In a public space there are hundreds of people wearing backpacks or carrying briefcases and suitcases. Look out for anyone who seems particularly nervous or who is looking around furtively. No matter how fanatical terrorists might be, they are likely to show normal human signs of tension and nervousness. After all, if they are suicide bombers, they are just about to blow themselves up. They will probably be anxious that the bomb might go off at the wrong time, before they are in position. They may be concerned that wires have been disconnected. They may be unusually nervous about people around them or anyone bumping into them. They may look warily at any officials and steer well clear of police or police dogs. If it is hot and most people are wearing minimum clothing, they may appear over-dressed and be sweating as well as nervous.

Terrorist targets

Terrorists will either make attacks on large numbers of innocent civilians in order to create shock and raise their profile and status, or they will target particular individuals because of their connections to governments, military forces, news organizations or commercial companies. Attacks in the first category include the World Trade Center attack, the Madrid train killings and the London transport bombings. Attacks in the second category include ongoing kidnappings of British, American and other nationals working for commercial organizations in countries such as Iraq, news reporters who venture into dangerous territory and ongoing attacks against military targets. There is no way of predicting what the warped mind of the terrorist will consider as a suitable target. For example, a member of a British charitable aid group was kidnapped and assassinated in Iraq.

KIDNAPPING AND HOSTAGE TAKING

If you are travelling to or already work in a high-risk area of the world, you need to brief yourself fully with all relevant government security information. Follow any professional security advice stringently. Travel along designated routes to and from work, but try to vary your routine so that your movements cannot be easily predicted. If you use a car, make sure that it is checked regularly for any form of tampering.

If a particular region has foreign forces involved and you are a national of those foreign countries, you are automatically a potential target for kidnapping and hostage taking. The hostage taking may take place because the terrorists wish to lead public opinion towards demanding a withdrawal of foreign troops from the region. They may want to use a hostage as a bargaining counter for the release of prisoners from their own group, or they may seek to raise money in exchange for your release, so that they can buy arms and other equipment to fund their cause.

You may be taken hostage in a variety of ways:
- From your car, following a road block or carjacking
- From your home.
- While walking down the street.
- From another location.

Dealing with a hostage crisis

Always be ready to escape potential hostage takers, but do not resist if directly threatened with a weapon.

Sometime the terrorists may pose as officials, at a roadblock, for example. Many Western governments have a policy of giving no concessions to terrorists and hostage takers and will not even openly negotiate with them. A deal may, however, be struck behind the scenes via undercover security

agencies. Most Western governments will take whatever active measures are possible and necessary to secure your release.

From the moment you are taken hostage, the security services, which will include intelligence, police and military units, will be on the case to try to identify where you are and, once that has been achieved, to undertake a rescue operation.

Minimizing the risk of being taken hostage

As described in the early chapters of this book, mental imagery and acting out what you would do in a hostage scenario will help to prepare you mentally for the unexpected, when there will be no time to think. If you have rehearsed the movements, you may have a chance of getting away.

Be vigilant all the time, especially if you are in a dangerous country, and use your native instincts of fight or flight. Take note if a car is slowing down and respect any warning voices in your mind that say that something is not quite right.

Do not carry bags, wallets or anything that will attract attention. You can fight to get free from someone who tries to grab you. If you are on the street and have not been captured, you still have a chance to get away – run and call for help. The hostage-takers do not want to be exposed in public for long.

If there is no chance of escape, be cooperative and do what you are told. The hostage-takers are likely to be nervous and may harm you if you do not comply with their wishes. Be clear and honest if you give any information, but otherwise be a 'grey' person.

Do not comment on any other hostages or give away information

TIP: ESCAPE FROM KIDNAPPERS

British special forces are trained to be aware that their best chance of escape is in the early stages of capture.

- If you have to walk to the place where you will be held captive, keep a look out for opportunities to escape, such as down a gully or into woods.
- If the hostage-takers have other hostages or if they are tired, they may not waste much time trying to chase you.
- If you take action, make sure it is decisive.
- Get into cover as soon as possible and keep going.

about them that may compromise their position.

Do not make comments that highlight your status, wealth, or political or religious opinions. Put yourself across as a normal, decent upright person. Remain observant without giving away any signs that you are observing. Accept food and drink when it is given to you, as you will need to maintain your strength if there is an opportunity to escape. You need to prepare yourself for a feat of endurance, as you may be held captive for a long period while the terrorists try to get what they want.

Keeping yourself going

If taken hostage, try to set yourself mental and physical routines that will keep both your mind and body in shape. Some hostages report remembering happy occasions with their families to keep their spirits up. Another hostage spent time planning trips with his family. You may remember favourite stories, recite poems or say prayers to yourself. Maintain a regime of stretching muscles and taking whatever exercise may be appropriate, such as press-ups or sit-ups, in order to keep your body in condition. Do not give up hope.

Hostage rescue scenario

Once the security services have identified where you are being held,

Hijacker techniques

Hijackers will often disorientate their victims by blinfolding them, so that they cannot easily track where they are being taken or what the time is.

Mental routines

Rigorous mental self-discipline will help you to survive long periods of captivity. Keep your thoughts positive by setting yourself mental exercises.

they will usually plan a rescue operation. The rescue operation will most likely involve forced entry into the building where you are being held, accompanied by stun grenades and accurate gunfire. It is vital that you do not get caught in the line of fire, as the security forces have to make split-second decisions about likely targets and may not immediately recognize you as a hostage. Remain on the ground unless otherwise directed by security personnel. Do exactly what they say.

Rescuers will perform search everyone and will probably handcuff both terrorists and hostages until a positive identification has been made.

Do not resist security personnel if they handcuff you or treat you in a rough manner.

Hostage rescue on an aircraft
If security personnel have to storm an

Assault team

Highly trained teams make violent forced entries. Do not get caught in the crossfire. The man at the front is carrying a ram bar to smash down doors, while the remainder of the team carry assorted weapons, including automatic pistols, assault rifles and short barrelled shotguns. The shotgun is used for shooting out door hinges and locks.

aircraft held by terrorists, they will have very little room for manoeuvre and will need to make snap decisions about shooting terrorists. If you are a passenger in such a scenario, keep your head well down below the level of the headrest so that you are not identified as a potential terrorist and so that you do not interfere with a soldier's line of sight when firing. Remain still until positively ordered to move by security personnel.

Special forces rescue

Your rescuers will have to make split-second decisions about friend and foe. Keep down and do exactly what you are told.

117

CRISIS IN THE HOME

Although there is no place like home, an alarming number of accidents, many of them fatal, occur in and around the home. These accidents can be the result of:

- Falls
- Accidental poisoning
- Drowning, suffocation or choking
- Fires

Falls

Surprisingly, one of the highest causes of fatalities in the home is falling – for example, falling downstairs, out of windows or off ladders. In the bathroom, falls can happen because of slippery floors as well as around obviously wet areas like showers and bathtubs. Even the slightest amount of movement in a shower can cause you to slip; the same can happen in the bath. Floors become wet through direct water spillage and through condensation.

Fall prevention in the home

Particularly if you have elderly relatives or young children in the house, you will need to put in extra safety equipment. Place a handrail on the stairway and child safety gates at the base and head of the stairs. Make sure stairways are well lit, particularly stairs going into otherwise dark areas such as a cellar. Do not use any rugs at the top of the stairs that are likely to slip on smooth floors, or which are likely to ruck up so that they can be tripped over.

To prevent falls from windows, particularly for younger children and babies, you will need to consider putting in window guards on upper floors, and on lower floors as well if there is a substantial drop or dangerous surface outside. Window guards need to be properly installed so that they do not suddenly give way when leant upon. It is possible to obtain removable window guards, which can be taken out easily if

Safety stair treads

A large number of falls and injuries happen on stairs. Non-slip treads make stairs safer.

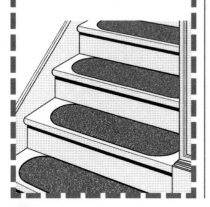

there is a fire and you need an escape route.

Ladders

Chairs are designed for sitting on, not standing on. Many falls in the home happen because people either use inappropriate equipment when reaching for things or they use the appropriate equipment but in the wrong way.

When using a ladder:
- Make sure it has a secure contact with the ground and will not slip.
- Make sure it is at the right angle.

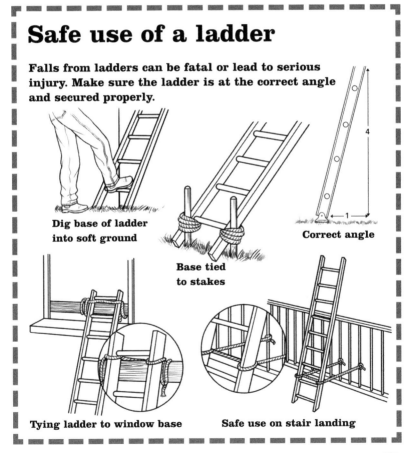

Safe use of a ladder

Falls from ladders can be fatal or lead to serious injury. Make sure the ladder is at the correct angle and secured properly.

Dig base of ladder into soft ground

Base tied to stakes

Correct angle

Tying ladder to window base

Safe use on stair landing

- Wear appropriate non-slip shoes.
- Do not stand on the top rung (individual ladders may have different safety recommendations for their use).
- Make sure the ladder is properly locked if it is a step ladder or lockable ladder.
- Do not place a ladder near cables.
- Keep yourself centred on the ladder. Do not be tempted to reach over to the side – come down and move the ladder closer to what you want to reach.

Poisons

Any poisonous materials, which may include products such as cleaning fluids and medicines, should be kept in cupboards that cannot be reached by young children, or in locked areas. To avoid accidental gas poisoning, install a carbon monoxide detector.

Water Hazards
Swimming pools

If children are around, swimming pools should either be fenced off with a locked gate when the pool is not in use or there should be an adult present at all times.

Bathtubs

Do not leave young children alone in the bath, and do not leave young children in a bath in the care of older children who are also in the bath. When filling a bathtub, do not fill it with water from the hot tap first. Fill the bath with cold water and then add hot or, if using a mixer tap, mix to an appropriate temperature that will not scald a child.

Suffocation and Choking Hazards

Do not leave soft toys inside a baby cot – the baby's face might become pressed into the toy, smothering the child. For similar reasons, do not hang over a cot mobiles that can be pulled down by the baby, and do not leave small objects lying around that can be picked up and eaten by a small child.

SAFETY ON THE STREET

The urban environment is full of potential hazards. These include everyday hazards such as walking under ladders and crossing the road, to crime-related hazards such as robbery and assault. The best way to ward off potential hazards is preparation and awareness, as well as common sense.

When you leave your home, office or other location, be aware of how long you plan to be out and take with you whatever you might need, including money, a mobile telephone and clothing suitable for the current weather conditions or any changes in the weather. An emergency could arise simply because you were out longer than expected and nobody

Being aware

In secluded and unfamiliar areas, keep a watchful eye out for suspicious people.

could get in touch with you. When you leave, let somebody know your likely route of travel and when you plan to return.

Depending on the threat level in the area in which you live, it is always a good idea to walk with your hands free in case you need to defend yourself. Remain alert at all times and do not wear an MP3 player, as it will prevent you from hearing suspicious noises, shouted warnings and the sound of approaching cars, motorcycles or bicycles.

Safe routes

When walking through an area, whether it is familiar or unfamiliar, keep to well-lit streets and places where there are other people going about their business. Do not take short-cuts down restricted alleyways, especially at night, or in areas where you are completely out of sight. Steer clear of areas where you see people acting suspiciously or looking for trouble. When walking down a road, choose the side of the pavement opposite to the flow of traffic if possible, in order to avoid kerb crawlers. If you know you will have to walk in unlit areas, carry a reliable torch. It is worth investing in a more expensive torch, as these tend to be more reliable and do not soak up battery power when not in use. Furthermore, you can use a metal torch as an improvised weapon if you are attacked.

Especially if you are a woman, carry an alarm system with you or an emergency whistle. The use of these may distract and confuse a potential assailant, allowing you enough time to get away. If you are walking in a particularly secluded area or where there are suspicious-looking people about, carry the alarm in your hand so that you can use it instantly where necessary.

If you are carrying a bag such as a handbag, keep the clasp close to your body so that a pickpocket cannot open it easily. Keep other essential items, such as house keys and perhaps a mobile phone, somewhere else about your person, so that if your bag is snatched you can get back into your house and/or phone for help.

If possible, avoid situations and people where violence is likely to occur. Keep away from bars where there are signs of noisy and aggressive behaviour. If you are on the street, avoid the entrances to bars or other places where young men may be drinking. If you are walking down the street and you see a group of individuals behaving suspiciously or in a rowdy mood, take a detour.

Action when being followed

If you sense someone is following you, check that it is safe to cross the road and then cross over. Do not panic and run in front of a car. If

Awareness on public transport

Beware of showing high tech and valuable equipment in public areas, which might attract unwelcome attention. Remain alert at all times – always be aware of those around you.

the person crosses over and continues to follow you, cross the road again, checking it is safe. They may give up. If there are other people around, get into a group of people and explain what is happening. Alternatively, go into a public place where you can find someone who can help you or call for help. If necessary, call the police, or any friends or relatives

who can come out to pick you up. Do not use a phone box in the street, as you could be trapped there by a pursuer.

SELF-DEFENCE

However fit or well trained you are in personal defence, you will always want to avoid a violent confrontation if possible. Awareness and preparation will help you to steer

123

Keep a safe distance

An open-handed guard position enables you to keep your distance and defend yourself if necessary. You can disguise the guard position (right).

clear of violent situations. Your body language will also help you to deter attack. Like animals, humans have a sixth sense for detecting somebody who is vulnerable. A person who wants to steal your handbag or your laptop does not wish to get into a fight, so they will choose someone who is less likely to fight.

If you follow the advice in the early chapters of this book and maintain a regular fitness regime, including weight training, your body will send out signals to a potential assailant that are likely to be off-putting. An athletic, strong person naturally holds himself well and walks in a way that exudes confidence.

Your physique may be visibly strong. A bully or potential thief will not want to try it on with someone who is likely to resist.

Threatening behaviour

Confrontations erupt over all kinds of things, especially where alcohol is involved. Most do not lead to violence, and of those that do, many could have been prevented. The key is to remain calm and not allow yourself to be drawn into an escalating confrontation, and never to allow anyone to get close to you while in an aggressive, confrontational state.

Signs of vulnerability
- Rounded or hunched shoulders and a manner of walking that suggests you wish your head would disappear between your shoulder blades.
- Crossed arms and/or legs that suggest evasive self-protection by minimizing the area of visible body surface. It also makes you seem less strong.
- Hands hovering around the face area, suggesting nervousness or uncertainty.
- Erratic, hurried body movements.
- A weak, tentative smile that shows eagerness to please.
- Eyes looking down at the ground or which dart around.
- Detachment from a peer group – a sense of isolation from the 'herd'.

Defensive posture

To adopt a defensive posture, keep your body angled away from the aggressor, one leg behind, balancing easily on slightly bent knees. Keep the forward hand up to deter blows and the rear hand ready to retaliate.

Signs of confidence and strength

- An upright, open stance.
- A steady gaze, straight ahead and not looking down.
- Arms hanging evenly by your side with fingers together.
- Calm, steady manner of speaking.
- Steady, deliberate body movements.
- Smiling only when necessary.
- An easy and open manner with other people.

If someone confronts you, they will be assessing your body language all the time. From your perspective, the signs of an impending attack are:

- Bulging eyes staring directly at you if they are drunk or very angry, or a calculated smile.
- Standing close to you in a threatening way.
- Aggressive questions.
- Finger pointing and head thrusting.
- Disrupted breathing due to surge of adrenaline and aggression.
- A deep breath just before he launches an attack.

If you are physically attacked by an aggressor, you have the right to use proportionate force to defend yourself. Afterwards, you may need to prove in a court of law that the force you used was proportionate, especially if the aggressor sustains a serious injury. Proportionate force means applying enough force to defend yourself, protect your relations or property and get away from danger.

You may wish to undergo some professional self-defence training. Even if you are trained in self-defence, the outcome of an attack is likely to be unpredictable and the assailant is unlikely to act in precisely the way for which you have been trained. You need therefore to be prepared for anything and to be adaptable in your response.

Defusing attackers

To attempt to defuse a potential attack, face the attacker with an open expression. Make a confident attempt to meet them halfway, acknowledging that there is a problem and perhaps even extending a hand to shake on it. If, however, they are determined to have a fight, you have no option other than to get away or to defend yourself.

Attack and run

If you are right-handed, step forwards with your left leg and create an angle of 45° to your opponent. Raise your open hands up to the front to create a protective zone. Open hands are not as immediately threatening and in fact suggest conciliation, but they will let you ward off the assailant's attack and you can bunch them into fists to strike a blow if necessary.

Your best defence is to keep clear of and ward off blows. Focus your eyes on the assailant's sternum, which will enable you to see the widest range of their movements.

Once under attack, bunch your fists and raise them to both sides of your jaw as a guard. If you get a punch through, return the fists immediately to the side of your jaw to maintain your protection. Jump diagonally away from any kicks and roll your head away from any punches to your face. If you manage to stun your opponent or put him off balance with a blow, take the opportunity to get away.

SAFETY ON TRANSPORT
Travelling by bus

As with all urban safety, be aware, plan and prepare when taking a public bus. Make sure you know your route and have enough money to get there and back. Do not hang around deserted bus stops or where there are suspicious people about or people who have obviously had too much to drink. If the bus is empty or if there is someone suspicious or threatening aboard, make sure you sit close to the driver. Have a mobile phone and a safety alarm to hand when approaching a bus stop on foot or when leaving the bus.

If you do not have the bus fare, do not attempt to find your way on foot unless you know the area well. Do not accept a lift or help from a stranger. If necessary, call a friend or family member and explain that you are stranded.

Travelling by taxi

Always use a reputable taxi firm and check that the taxi that arrives is the one your ordered. The driver should carry the correct identification and be able to identify you. Do not fall asleep in the taxi, and if you are unsure of the driver's intent ask to be dropped off in a well-lit area.

Travelling by train

Travelling by train is relatively safe. Modern trains often have CCTV in the carriages so the guard can see what is going on at all times. Yet some precautions are necessary.

When waiting for a train at the platform, make sure you stand in a well-lit area. Keep on the lookout for anyone suspicious and remain in a group of sensible-looking people if possible. When you get on the train, do not sit in a carriage on your own if possible, and also avoid groups of rowdy or intimidating individuals.

If necessary, find out where the guard is located and sit near there. It is preferable to choose a seat where you are close to a door or have a compartment barrier behind you, so that you can see everyone before you and no one can approach from behind.

If disruptive or suspicious people get on the train, move to another carriage or contact the guard. Try not to fall asleep on a train, as this will make you extremely vulnerable to pickpockets or attack and you may also miss your stop.

Railway accidents

Train accidents are rare, but make sure you read the safety advice on board the train before or soon after the train sets off, and be aware of any emergency equipment. If the train is involved in an accident, the signs will be heavy braking, a rocking motion or a pitching sensation as the train comes off the tracks. Lean forwards with your head towards your knees and put your arms over your head. If you have a coat, use it to cover your head to protect yourself from flying objects and glass.

Unless there is any immediate danger, the best option is to remain on the train once it has come to a halt, as there may be several other hazards on the track, such as moving trains, electric rails or electric cables that may have fallen. If you do have to get out, use the doors if they will open or emergency equipment provided, such as glass hammers, to break through the windows.

Do not cross rail tracks unless you are specifically ordered to do so by an emergency official or unless

Know your escape route

If you feel threatened, make sure you have a clear exit plan. Note who gets on and off the train, and survey the platform before you step out yourself.

you are sure you have correctly identified electric rails.

In the event of a rail crash

Although train travel is relatively safe, accidents occasionally occur due either to human error, a failure of technology or through deliberate sabotage, such as a terrorist bombing. Modern trains are designed to withstand huge impacts, have carefully-designed interiors with a minimum of sharp edges and incorporate such safety features as pressurized glass. The negative effect of this is that sometimes it may prove difficult to get out of some parts of a crashed train or for rescuers to get in.

If the train is involved in a crash, follow any instructions that may come through the intercom or directly from the driver or guard. Use any emergency warnings that may be available and if it is safe to evacuate the train use the specified exits or window-breaking equipment. If rescuers are on the scene, follow their instructions and do not waste time looking for personal belongings.

If you do need to leave the train for whatever reason, be aware of such dangers as the powered third rail, which can cause instant death through electrocution, or downed power lines. You will also need to be aware of any combustible materials such as diesel fuel. If the accident has only just occurred, other trains may not be aware of it and there is a danger of trains travelling through on the same line or adjacent lines and causing a secondary accident.

Underground train crashes

If you are involved in an accident in an underground train, it may be more difficult to leave the train and get to safety. You should follow the instructions of staff at all times, move away from any immediate danger, open windows for ventilation and remain on the train

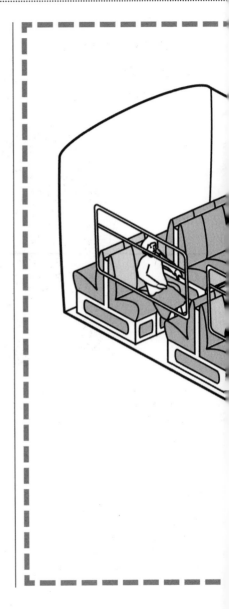

Train crash

In a train crash, it is often safest to remain on board until rescued – unless there is a fire or other hazard. Do not attempt to force open damaged doors, as these could be unstable and cause an injury.

MAJOR TRAIN ACCIDENTS
(150 DEATHS OR MORE)

1700+ Queen of the Sea train disaster (Sri Lanka, 2004) ; part of 2004 Indian Ocean Earthquake.

800–1000 (France, 1917).

575 (Russia, 1989).

521–600+ (Italy, 1944).

428 (Awash, Afar, Ethiopia, 1985).

383 (Egypt, 2002).

337 (Azerbaijan, 1995).

320 (Iran, 2004).

307 (Sindh, Pakistan, 1990).

302 (India, 1995).

300+ (Mexico, 1955).

298 (Costa Rica, 1926).

285 (India, 1999).

268 (Bihar, India, 1981).

236 (Buenos Aires, Argentina, 1970).

230 (France, 1933).

227 (Scotland, 1915).

212 (India, 1998).

208 (Mexico, 1972).

196 (Mozambique, 2002).

186 (Genthin, Germany, 1939).

185 (Aracaju, Sergipe, Brazil, 1946).

184 (Komagawa, Saitama, Japan, 1947).

162 (Tokyo, Japan, 1962).

161 (Japan, 1963).

159 (Rzepin, Slubice, Poland, 1952).

155 (Austria, 2000).

154 (North Korea, 2004).

153 (Croatia, 1974).

151 (New Zealand, 1953).

150 (KwaZulu Natal, South Africa, 1965).

unless specifically instructed to leave. If emergency lighting does not work, use whatever light you have available, such as a torch, mobile phone or lighted watch.

Travelling by car

Make sure your car is regularly serviced and carry out regular checks yourself on the tyres. (Do a visual check for obvious signs of a flat tyre and for any bulges in the tyre wall or nails or other sharp objects sticking into the tyre; also check the pressure with a tyre gauge). Before setting off on a journey, also check the vehicle's water (both engine coolant and windscreen washers) and oil levels. It is a good idea to have emergency equipment stowed safely in the car at all times.

Plan your route carefully. Take any necessary maps and make sure someone knows about your expected time of arrival. If you are

Dangerous routes

When travelling by car in dangerous areas, keep moving and keep your windows up and doors locked.

TIP: SPARE CAR EQUIPMENT CHECKLIST

- First aid kit
- Warning triangle (this is not always supplied by the car manufacturer)
- Car jack
- High-visibility safety vests (a legal requirement in some countries)
- A reliable torch
- Spare car light bulbs (a legal requirement in some countries)
- Spare water (for topping up the car and for passengers)
- Spare oil
- Spare fuel in a fuel can (for longer journeys)
- A blanket and waterproof ground sheet
- Rope for towing
- Jump leads

on a remote road or somewhere at night that is unfamiliar or badly lit, do not stop if somebody flags you down. If there seems to have been an accident, phone for help or drive to the nearest place where you can find assistance. Do not pick anyone up you do not know.

When driving in a town or city, keep doors locked in case someone should try to enter the car. If you need to wind down the window to speak to someone, make sure it is only a crack and not enough for someone to put a hand through the opening. When stopping or parking, choose a place that is well lit or where there is space around you so that you can see if anyone is approaching. If you are uneasy or if you see someone suspicious approaching, get back in the car and drive away.

Carjacking

This crime involves criminals stealing your car while you are using it. Carjacking is carried out in a number of different ways. Criminals may pose as flower sellers or offer a car-cleaning service in order to get you to stop. Once you have stopped to speak to them, they may force their way into the car. Alternatively, criminals will set up a fake accident or flat tyre scenario and flag you down for help. When you get out of the car, they take your keys and steal the vehicle. Carjackers may also catch you unawares when you are parking, as your observation levels are often low at such times.

If faced with any of these situations, do not stop. Steer round

Car jacking

If you are threatened with guns or knives by car jackers, it is better to hand over the car than risk injury or death.

any obstacles, or reverse if it is safe to do so. Keep the doors locked and the windows closed. If you are completely blocked in and the carjackers have weapons, it is better to lose your car than get injured or killed. An average family car is not proof against bullets.

If someone bumps into the back of your car with another car, do not stop to remonstrate but drive away from the scene as quickly and as safely as possible and report the

incident to the police. If you are confronted with an aggressive driver – even in ordinary circumstances – do not get out of your vehicle or open your window. It is better to drive off and report the incident if necessary.

Driver awareness

The safest driver is someone who is fully aware of what is going on around him or her and is paying complete attention to the dynamics

Safe removal of cyclist's helmet

If you think a cyclist who has been knocked down by a vehicle may have fractured their neck, keep their head and neck stable when you remove their helmet, as shown.

of the car and the ever-changing scene around him. The obvious point is to be aware of basic rules of driving, including maintaining a safe distance from the vehicle in front of you. Do not 'tailgate' – you could run into the vehicle in front of you if it should suddenly slow down, or you could cause an aggressive reaction, or 'road rage', in the driver ahead. Some drivers, when annoyed that someone is too close, deliberately jab their brakes on. Alternatively, an annoyed driver may allow you to overtake and then aggressively tailgate you, flashing his lights.

Consider taking an advanced driving course, which will teach you better ways of handling a car in a variety of different conditions and will also equip you to better handle an emergency.

Road accidents

If you have hit another vehicle or a pedestrian, make sure you stop in a safe way and in a safe place that is not likely to cause another accident. Use hazard warning flashers on your car and any other safety equipment, such as wearing a high-visibility jacket. Immediately assess whether someone has been hurt (in which case administer first aid and/or call an ambulance). If the accident has caused a road obstruction and there is a danger to other road users, immediately call

TIP: EXCHANGING DETAILS IN AN ACCIDENT

Obtain the name, address, telephone number, vehicle registration, insurance company and insurance policy number of other drivers involved. Provide your own information to the other parties. Take a photograph of the scene if you have a camera or camera phone or make a sketch, taking down names of roads and streets nearby and details of vehicles involved, including make and colour.

the police and give clear and accurate details of your location.

Breakdowns

If your car breaks down, pull onto the hard shoulder to the far left (in countries which use the left-hand side of the road) with your wheels turned to the left. Put on your hazard flashers and keep sidelights on. Get out of the car and keep well to the side of the road. Do not stand behind the car. Wear safety reflective vests if available, and put out a warning triangle only if you are not on a motorway/freeway – but make sure it does not cause an obstruction in the road.

Call for help on an emergency telephone or mobile. If you are alone and feel threatened, wait in the vehicle with the driver's door locked.

Travelling by airplane

Although air travel is mostly a pleasurable and exciting experience, often associated with visiting new places or embarking on an expedition, it can also be fraught with complications and dangers.

Online check-in facilities and advanced airport terminal facilities make the process of travel and checking-in much easier. Ensure that you have all the necessary documentation, including visas, and that your passport is valid for the entire period you will be away (taking into account that some countries demand that a passport should have at least six months before its expiry date at the time of travel).

Find out from the airline or government information services what other documentation you may need. Make sure you have all the necessary medial inoculations and insurance. It is important to double-check details such as:

- Flight number

- The airline (bearing in mind the plane could be sub-leased to anopther carrier)
- The scheduled departure time
- The departure terminal and location of the correct short- or long-term car parks
- Your baggage allowance

Pack your bags carefully and be careful about what you take in your cabin luggage, as certain objects and liquids may be confiscated at the airport.

Bags

Your bags should carry clear labelling both inside and outside, displaying your destination address, e-mail address and mobile phone number. Do not carry sharp objects, including pen knives, in your hand luggage. You will probably not be allowed to carry any form of liquids, including bottled water, through airport security.

Especially for long-haul flights, you may encounter problems associated with dehydration and with sitting in a relatively confined space for long periods. To minimize the effects of dehydration, do not consume too much alcohol, and make sure you drink enough water during the flight.

Dehydration

The human body is made up of about 70 per cent water, and therefore any conditions that affect the balance of water in the body will have a negative

Be aware of exits

Take note of emergency exits on board an aircraft; this will allow you to react quickly in an emergency and reach the exit point safely and with the minimum of fuss.

TIP: EXERCISE TO REDUCE THE RISK OF DEEP-VEIN THROMBOSIS

You can perform exercises while seated that will help to keep your circulation going and reduce the risk of developing a deep-vein thrombosis.
• Raise your heels, keeping your toes on the floor, then bring them down again. Do this 10 times.
• Raise and lower your toes 10 times.
Perform these exercises every 30 minutes or so in addition to moving around the plane when it is appropriate to do so.

mean that the body will work less effectively, and it can normally be put right by drinking more water. Dehydration is not normally identified by feeling thirsty. Symptoms of dehydration include a slight headache, dry eyes and dizziness. An accurate test of low water content in your body is when you visit the lavatory and find your urine is a dark colour. The colour should be relatively clear. If you have these symptoms, drink more water.

Infection transfer
The closed environment of an aircraft and its re-circulated air means that there is a higher chance of infection being spread from one passenger to another. You may wish to consider increasing your intake of vitamins such as Vitamin C, which can help boost your immune system, or other natural medications.

It is said that a saline spray can keep your nasal passages lubricated, reducing the risk of an airborne infection taking hold. On some aircraft, you can adjust the flow of air above your head to keep yourself cool.

High blood pressure
The stress associated with travel and with fear of flying can increase your blood pressure. If you are unfit or have a weight problem, stress and high blood pressure can become serious issues. Take medical advice if you have a particular issue with fear

effect. Water also acts as a lubricant for eyes and joints, helps digestion, keeps the skin pores clear and flushes out toxins.

Dehydration occurs when there is at least a 1 per cent loss of body weight due to lack of fluid. Mild dehydration at this level will just of flying and discuss how to reduce the side effects as far as possible.

Air rage and provocative or difficult passengers

Fellow passengers may have an attitude problem, have drunk too much alcohol, have experienced difficulties with their travel arrangements or just be plain aggressive for no good reason at all. In view of the confined space aboard an aircraft, it is better not to confront such people, some of whom will welcome the opportunity for a fight. To avoid such people, take a look at the passengers before you board the aircraft and make note of any who may be argumentative or rowdy. If you find that you are due to be seated near such people, notify the airline staff and register a complaint. Even if the person or people in question are not moved or kept off the aircraft, the airline staff and/or cabin crew will be alerted in advance to the potential problem.

Do not become argumentative and aggressive yourself, otherwise you may be identified by the airline staff or cabin crew as a troublemaker, which will make it more difficult to maintain their sympathy and assistance if there is a problem.

Spotting a troublemaker

Maintain your vigilance during the flight and notify cabin staff confidentially if you think a problem is developing with a passenger or group of passengers. Remember, people who are in an aggressive frame of mind are often looking for someone to oppose them so that they can vent their frustrations. Do not provide them with the opportunity. If you react to the aggression, however innocent you may be, you become part of the problem. Airline cabin crew are trained to identify potential troublemakers themselves and any suspicious behaviour or troublesome people. The best course of action, therefore, is to leave the air crew to do their job and intervene yourself only if absolutely necessary, such as defending yourself from an unprovoked attack from someone who is out of control. If the situation becomes violent and, for example, a member of the cabin staff is being overpowered, you should use minimum force to help until other cabin crew arrive. Otherwise, keep your distance and do not look in the direction of a troublemaker, let alone stare at him. Do not allow anyone with you to become involved either, and if you are with children do not let them stare at a troublemaker or make comments.

Surprisingly, training for air rage incidents is not always consistent among airlines despite the fact that the problem is increasing significantly at the time of writing.

Air rage

If confronted with air rage, maintain an assertive defensive posture so that you do not become part of the problem.

Remember, however, that the cabin crew have the power to enforce existing legislation with regard to disruption on board the plane and will inform the necessary authorities on the ground. They can refuse to carry a disruptive passenger on the next leg of a journey and ban him or her from future flights. This power should deter disruptive passengers. Make sure that you remain on the right side of the law and do only the minimum to defend yourself if necessary.

Dealing with a hi-jack crisis
Although the hijacking of a plane is a rare event, especially in view of heightened security after 9/11, it is

well to be prepared in case it does occur. The hijackers will normally be heavily outnumbered by the crew and passengers and they are likely to act violently and defensively to establish their dominance. Remain calm and do not attract attention to yourself. Do not catch their eye and remain as grey as possible, giving minimal answers to questions. Advise people around you to also remain calm.

Comply with instructions given by the hijackers unless they involve harming other people. Prepare yourself mentally for what may be a long and arduous experience as the plane may be diverted and passengers required to stay on board while the hijackers negotiate with authorities on the ground.

While remaining grey, also be aware of what is going on around you and especially of any increase in tension that may signal a rescue attempt. If special forces storm the plane, keep your head down, with your hands behind your neck. Do not raise your head or try to identify yourself unless security personnel order you to do so. Security forces will need to positively clear you before you are released.

Turbulence

Aircraft may enter unexpected areas of air turbulence. Turbulence is due to a number of causes, including atmospheric pressure, jet streams, cold or warm fronts and thunderstorms. Air pockets are probably the most common form of turbulence and cause the aeroplane to feel like a car on a bumpy road.

The crew should be the first individuals aware of impending air turbulence and should notify the passengers. Make sure you do not ignore the advice and return to your seat promptly. The highest incidence of injuries to both passengers and crew in air turbulence incidents is to those not wearing seatbelts. The seat belt keeps you effectively anchored to the aircraft, so that you move with it, whereas if you are standing or sitting without a seat belt you are likely to be thrown around.

Stay put

Light turbulence may mean that you are able to move safely back to your seat with a few minor jolts. Hang on to seat edges as you move. If you are seated, you will strain a bit against your seat belt without undue discomfort. Moderate turbulence means you should be in your seat with your seatbelt on at all times, and be aware of the danger of objects being dislodged in the aircraft.

Severe turbulence will cause violent movements in the plane and may even cause significant changes in the plane's direction and its altitude in flight. Under such circumstances, you will find it impossible to walk in the cabin.

Turbulence

Turbulence in aircraft can be unexpected and potentially dangerous if you are not wearing a seat belt.

Aircraft crashes

About 2.5 billion people are carried in planes every year at immense speeds at altitudes of around 9000m (30,000ft). Air travel is surprisingly safe and even in crashes, there is a high chance of survival.

Your chances of survival will increase if you are well prepared both physically and mentally. Be aware of all safety exits and listen carefully to safety instructions before the flight. There will be little time to search for life jackets if there is an emergency. If you are visiting the lavatory, get a feel for where the nearest emergency exit is and how you would get there quickly. Each aircraft is different, so do not take anything for granted. Consider what you wear when

Using the emergency chute

To escape swiftly, go from a standing position straight down the chute. Cross your arms before you jump.

- Do not stop and perch on the edge before launching yourself down the chute.

- Do not wear high heels or take baggage with you.

Aircraft evacuation routes

Most civil passenger aircraft have ample escape routes. They work well if everyone remains calm and follows safety instructions.

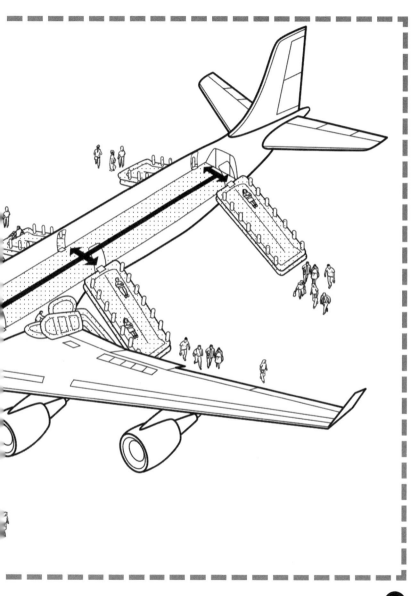

FOG—visibility less than 1km (0.5 nautical miles)

POOR—visibility between 1km and 3.7km (0.5–2 nautical miles)

MODERATE—visibility between 3.7km and 9.2km (2–5 nautical miles)

GOOD—visibility more than 9.2km (5 nautical miles)

travelling, and how you would move about a plane quickly in an emergency. High heels, for example, would not be helpful. Think also of the effectiveness of clothing if you have to move outside the plane. Wool and cotton are probably the best material and less likely to be affected by heat. The back of the plane is the safest place to sit and if you sit near the aisle you can obviously get out quicker. Leave all personal belongings behind if you have to leave the plane and put a damp cloth or handkerchief over your mouth if there is smoke in the cabin.

EMERGENCIES AT SEA

There are a vast number of activities associated with the sea, including coastal path walking and cliff climbing, surfing and windsurfing, sailing, motorboating and sport fishing. Whatever activity you are involved in, it is important to get the right training for the activity if it is in

Personal Flotation Devices

Floatation aid

or near the water and to make sure that you have all the right equipment, including safety equipment.

Clothing

Correct clothing at sea is even more important than on land, partly because it is generally colder at sea than it is on land. You should also carry extra clothing in case you are involved in an emergency. Anyone on a boat should wear a life jacket in case they find themselves in the water.

Weather conditions

Before venturing out in a boat, check the weather forecast. The Beaufort

It is a good idea to familiarize yourself with the different types of safety equipment, such as PFDs.

Life vest

Near shore bouyancy vest

Beaufort Scale
NB – 1 mile = 0.6km

No.	Knots	mph	Description
0	0	0mph	Calm
1	1–3	1–3mph	Light air
2	4–6	4–7mph	Light breeze
3	7–10	8–12mph	Gentle breeze
4	11–16	13–18mph	Moderate wind
5	17–21	19–24mph	Fresh wind
6	22–27	25–31mph	Strong wind
7	28–33	32–38mph	Very strong wind
8	34–40	39–46mph	Gale
9	41–47	47–54mph	Severe gale
10	48–55	55–63mph	Storm
11	56–63	64–72mph	Severe storm
12	63	73mph	Hurricane force

Effects at sea	Effects on land
Sea like a mirror	Smoke drifts in the wind
Ripples, but no foam crests	Leaves rustle; wind felt on face
Small wavelets	Small twigs in constant motion; light flags extended
Large wavelets crests, not breaking	Dust, leaves and loose paper raised; small branches move
Numerous whitecaps	Small trees sway
Many whitecaps, some spray	Large branches move; whistling in phone wires; difficult to use umbrellas
Larger waves form; whitecaps everywhere; more spray	Whole trees in motion
White foam from breaking waves begins to be blown in streaks	Twigs break off trees; difficult to walk
Edges of wave crests begin to break into spindrift	Chimney pots and slates removed
High waves; sea begins to roll; spray may reduce visibility	Trees uprooted; structural damage.
Very high waves with overhanging crests; blowing foam gives sea a white appearance	Widespread damage
Exceptionally high waves are filled with foam; sea completely white. Visibility greatly reduced.	Widespread damage; very rarely experienced on land.

Douglas Scale
Douglas sea and swell scale

SEA		LOW		MODERATE
	no swell	short or average	long	short
	0	1	2	3
0 calm	00	01	02	03
1 smooth	10	11	12	13
2 slight	20	21	22	23
3 moderate	30	31	32	33
4 rough	40	41	42	43
5 very rough	50	51	52	53
6 high	60	61	62	63
7 very high	70	71	72	73
8 precipitous	80	81	82	83
9 confused	90	91	92	93

SEA	HEAVY			
	short	average	long	swell
	6	7	8	9
0 calm	06	07	08	09
1 smooth	16	17	18	19
2 slight	26	27	28	29
3 moderate	36	37	38	39
4 rough	46	47	48	49
5 very rough	56	57	58	59
6 high	66	67	68	69
7 very high	76	77	78	79
8 precipitous	86	87	88	89
9 confused	96	97	98	99

average	long
4	5
04	05
14	15
24	25
34	35
44	45
54	55
64	65
74	75
84	85
94	95

Tidal currents can have an extreme effect on wave height. If the ebb tide is running against the wind direction, the waves can become very choppy.

TIP: ACTION FOR MAN OVERBOARD (MOB)

STOP – it is very difficult to see someone in the water, so try to remain as close to the spot they went in as possible.

MARK – throw out a lifebuoy and also some form of marker, such as a flare. GPS are sometimes equipped with an MOB button.

ALARM – call for help from other boats or from rescue services to locate and recover the MOB.

MANOEUVRE – there are set manoeuvres for turning a boat or ship back to the location of a MOB. In order for these to work, they need to be practised carefully.

RECOVER – you need to have the right equipment to recover a MOB from the water, bearing in mind that conditions may be rough and the MOB may be suffering from hypothermia.

Man overboard

If there is a man overboard, keep as close to the spot as possible. If you are in the water, shout, blow a whistle and signal with your hands.

Scale indicates the strength of the wind, while the Douglas Scale describes the state of the sea, indicating the height of the waves.

Fog

Fog is a well-known hazard at sea and has been the cause of many shipwrecks over the centuries. Fog is created by an excess amount of water vapour in the air.

When the air is cold, its capacity for holding water is reduced and the result is fog. When the air gets warmer (with the sun rising on a clear day), the fog should disperse as the air gradually absorbs more moisture.

Risk reduction

Emergencies at sea can result from a number of factors, including a

Rescue quoit

Alternative means of rescue include:

• **throwing out a life buoy with a rope;**

• **swimming with a life buoy;**

• **or simply swimming out wearing a life jacket and with a line.**

TIP:
IF YOU FALL IN
THE WATER

- Tighten up all the seals on your sleeves, ankles and collar.
- Use the light and whistle on the life jacket to attract attention.
- Cross your legs and hold your arms tightly together.
- Turn your back to any waves so as not to take in any seawater.

faulty engine, a man overboard (MOB), swamping or capsizing in rough seas, fire and a wreck on rocks or some other part of the shore.

To minimize the risk of problems caused by engine faults, make sure that your engine is regularly serviced and that you are well trained to deal with conventional faults. Take an engine manual with you on any journey.

To reduce the risk of a man overboard, make sure crew wear life jackets and that they also have a harness which can be clipped on. If someone falls overboard, especially

in rough conditions with poor visibility, they can be very difficult to find. Boat crews should practise MOB techniques so that they know exactly what to do in a crisis.

Fire on board

Fires on boats can have a number of causes, including the gases used for cooking, which can sometimes escape and become ignited by a spark. There are a variety of safety rules regarding gas appliances on boats, which should be followed stringently. Make sure the bilges of the boat, and any areas where gas is stored, are aired regularly. Also ensure you have the correct type of fire extinguishers for putting out gas fires.

Action in a fire

Move everyone to a safe part of the boat, taking the life raft with you. Batten down the hatches near the fire so that oxygen supply to the fire is reduced – open hatches only in so far as it is necessary to use a fire extinguisher effectively. Use a fire blanket to cover the fire if you can approach it safely, then move yourself and any crew upwind of the fire.

Use of a life raft

In an emergency, the life raft should be used only as a last resort. If your boat is still seaworthy, it is better to remain there. Before launching and entering the life raft, make sure you have all the essential supplies you will need, including distress flares, communication equipment and spare food, water and clothing. Life rafts are designed to be inflated in the water. Make sure the life raft remains attached to the boat until everyone is safely aboard.

Cut the painter attaching the life raft to the sinking boat. Stream the drogue and make sure the life raft is fully inflated. Check for and patch any leaks.

Distress signals

A number of distress signals can be used at sea.

- Raise and lower your arms from your sides to above your head.
- Learn the international distress flags and use them.

Abandoning a burning ship

When abandoning a burning boat or ship, launch your life raft well away from the flames and make sure the raft is not blown towards them.

Life raft

Ensure your life raft has a stock of essential safety supplies and survival aids, including first aid kit, signal flares and fishing lines.

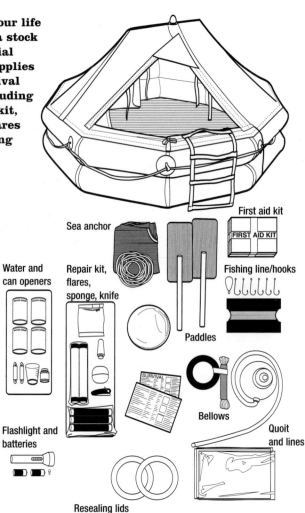

Sea anchor

First aid kit

FIRST AID KIT

Water and can openers

Repair kit, flares, sponge, knife

Fishing line/hooks

Paddles

Flashlight and batteries

SURVIVAL

Bellows

Quoit and lines

Resealing lids

Distress signals

Use distress signals to show you need help.

1. If you are in a dinghy, place your arms straight up by your sides and move them slowly up and down.

Or:

2. If you are in the water, place one arm straight up and wave it slowly side to side.

159

- Make smoke if this can be done safely on board.
- Whistles, horns and even guns can be used as distress signals. A gun should be fired about once per minute.
- Make sure you have a supply of flares, as these are a very effective means of signalling.

- Radios, GPS devices and electronic distress beacons (Emergency Position Indicating Radio Beacon – EPIRB) provide effective long-range distress signalling.

If a helicopter rescue is taking place, you may be instructed to hold a hand-held orange flare to

Launching a life raft

When launching a life raft, keep it attached to the boat with a painter while launching and inflating. Untie the painter promptly once safely aboard.

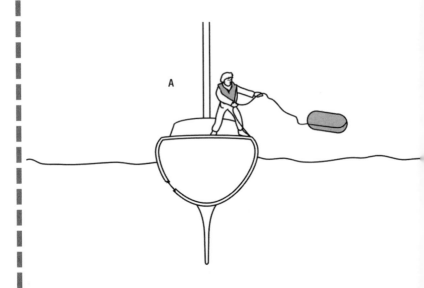

help the pilot position the helicopter. Do not fire any kind of flare in the vicinity of the helicopter, as this may damage the engines. Do not touch the line from the helicopter until the winchman has been lowered, and do not tie any line from the helicopter to a boat or dinghy.

Abandoning ship

If you are on a large boat or ship, follow all the instructions that are given on the voyage and make sure you know the way from your cabin to the life boat decks. If you have to jump off a sinking boat or ship, try to get as far away from it as possible: a powerful suction is created as water

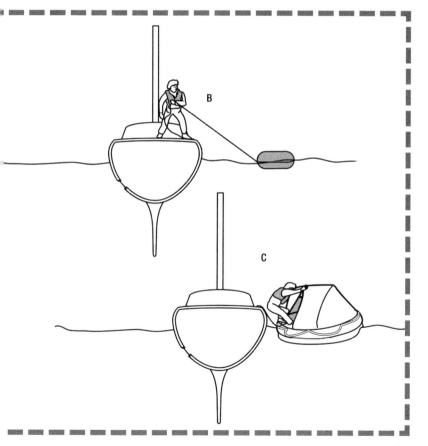

pours into the vacuum created by the sinking vessel – and if you are too close to the ship, you might be dragged down with it.

If there is an emergency on board, put on warm clothing, including waterproofs. Put on your life jacket, but do not inflate it before leaving the vessel. Take any essential safety items, such as flares or a torch. If you cannot get into a life boat on board the ship, jump into the water with legs straight and close together, one arm by your side and one hand covering your nose and mouth. Once you are in the water, you can inflate your life jacket. If you see a life boat or life raft, swim towards it by paddling your arms backwards, as if you were rowing a dinghy.

Using flares

Do not light flares on a life raft, since they could cause the raft to catch fire. Place them downwind of the raft so that you are not engulfed in smoke.

TIP:
HELP POSITION
(HEAT ESCAPE LESSENING POSTURE)

To increase your chances of survival in cold water, adopt the HELP position:

- Keep your arms tucked into your side to prevent heat loss from your sides.

- Cup your hand over your mouth and nose to keep water out.

- Cross your legs and keep them together to prevent heat loss from around your groin.

The shock of being cut off from civilization can be a major source of trauma. But remember that the circumstances you are in have been faced by men and women many times before. Although you may not be aware of it, you already have the inbuilt qualities to survive: determination, perseverance, resourcefulness and good humour.

DESERT SURVIVAL

There are more than 50 major deserts in the world. A desert usually has less than 25.4cm (10in) of annual rainfall and a high average temperature. Rain comes at irregular times and therefore cannot be easily predicted. Daytime temperatures can reach 55°C (131°F) in the shade, whereas at night temperatures are known to plummet to near freezing. The temperature range can be as great as 30°C (86°F).

There is a variety of desert terrains, including mountainous, rocky, sandy, salt marsh and wadi. Whatever the terrain, the desert is usually difficult to cross on foot, quite apart from the effects of the harsh sun.

Clothing

It is better to be clothed in the desert, despite the heat. Wear loose-fitting

....

Left: There are many techniques that can be learned to help you survive in the wilderness.

4

Wilderness survival requires an immediate strategy to deal with your new circumstances.

Crisis in the Wilderness

Crisis Situations

Desert dangers

clothing that will not stick to your flesh when you sweat and which will not absorb too much body sweat. Take a leaf out of the Arabs' book and wear a loose headdress that you can wrap around your face, if necessary, to protect the eyes, nose and mouth from glare reflected from the desert floor, from the sun above and from wind-blown sand and dust.

Although we are used to walking barefoot on a sandy beach, footwear must be worn in the desert. The sand will often be too

A desert environment during the day poses multiple dangers, including direct heat from the sun and reflected heat from the desert floor. Wear light, confortable clothing and good quality walking boots.

Shelters

If you are a victim of a plane or vehicle accident in the desert, you can shelter near to the wreckage, as this will increase the chances of being spotted by rescuers. The inside of an aircraft may, however, be too hot during the day.

As it is vital to reduce perspiration and preserve water, do not attempt to build a major shelter during the heat of the day. Improvise, if necessary, during the day and build a larger shelter during the cool of the evening. Rocky outcrops and caves can be good, cool places for shelters. Check for any insects or reptiles that might be sheltering there. As rainfall is unpredictable in a desert, do not build a shelter in a gully, to avoid the danger of drowning in a flash flood.

The type of shelter you build will depend on your location. You can stretch some canvas or a poncho from the top of a rocky outcrop or sand dune to the ground, weighing the ends down with rocks. Such a construction will make a reasonable temporary shelter to keep you out of the glare of the sun.

To make a more elaborate and cooler shelter, find a natural depression in the ground between rocks (not on an obvious water course) and weigh down your poncho to form a roof overhead. Alternatively, dig a trench that will have enough room for you and any equipment, and create a roof overhead with the

hot to walk on, and its dessicating effect will cause your feet to dry out, resulting in painful cracks. If you wear boots, you can keep sand out by fashioning a form of gaiter round the top of the boot with a piece of material.

Desert shelter

A sample shelter can provide the essential protection to survive the desert sun. Note the double-layer construction, which allows the outer layer to absorb the sun's heat while the inner layer remains cool.

poncho. To make it even more effective, and if you have two ponchos, create a double layer with 30–45cm (12–18in) of air space in between the two sheets.

Another way to construct a shelter is to set up four blocks of stone or sandbags, lay the single sheet or double poncho layer over the top and use a peg system with rope or string at all four corners for support.

Finding water

Water takes precedence over food in the desert, and it must be managed very carefully to ensure survival.

Be careful about the amount of food you eat, as you will need to

Water intake in 24-hour period during resting conditions			
Fahrenheit	**Centigrade**	**US/UK pints**	**Litres**
95°	35°	8½ / 7	4
90°	32°	6½ / 5¼	3
80°	27	2 / 1¾	1

Finding water

In dry river beds, water is most likely to be found in the lowest point on the outside of the bend.

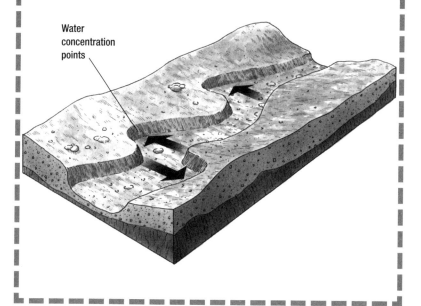

Water concentration points

drink more water to process the food. Avoid fatty foods, which absorb larger amounts of water than other types of food.

The Bushmen of the Kalahari sometimes obtain water by locating the deepest part of an old water course and digging down into the sand to arm's length until the sand is moist. Make a 1.5m (5ft) tube from the stem of a bush with a soft core, and insert it into the hole. Pack sand around it firmly. Then suck on the tube until water comes into your mouth.

You can extract water from wet sand or mud by putting the mud into a cloth and wringing out the water into a container. As a long-term technique, put out a tarpaulin to form a small reservoir so that any rain that falls is caught and flows to the centre.

Water from plants

The following plants can contain enough water to aid survival:

Cactus – cut the top off a barrel cactus. Extract water from the pulp by squeezing or mashing it, but do not eat the pulp.

Date palms – cut a low branch near the base and collect any liquid that oozes out.

Baobab tree – penetrate the large trunk to extract water.

TIP:
LOCATING WATER

- Look in valleys, gulleys and water courses, at the lowest point or the outside of the bend.
- Follow the tracks of birds and animals – they may lead to water.
- Look for any signs of greenery, especially palm trees.
- If you see signs of clouds or rain in the distance, head towards them.
- Look in the foot of cliffs or rock outcrops. Water may have collected in holes or depressions.
- Look in caves or fissures. Probe with a tube rather than your fingers, in case dangerous creatures are inside.
- Look out for man-made wells.
- If you find brackish water, try to locate the source spring.

TIP:
MAKING A SOLAR STILL

1. Dig a round hole approximately 1m (3ft) across and about 60cm (2ft) deep in an unshaded spot. Dig a hole for the container at the base.
2. Place one end of a tube in the container and pass the other end up to the lip of the hole.
3. Place a plastic sheet over the hole, covering the edges of the sheet to anchor it. Make sure the sheet does not touch the sides of the hole.
4. The sheet should droop about 40cm (16in) into the hole, but hang clear of the container.
5. Put a fist-sized stone in the centre of the sheet above the container.

Water should condense on the underside of the sheet and drip into the container. Within 24 hours, there should be about a pint of water in the container.

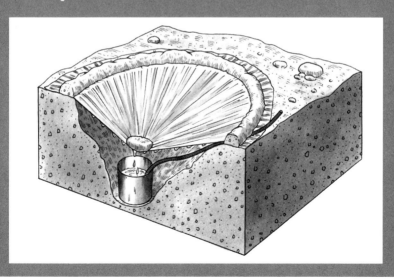

Rain trap

A simple construction involving two sticks and a large leaf can provide a trap for essential water.

Water from a cactus

Cut the head off a barrel cactus and extract water stored in the spongy tissue inside.

Cut the head

Insert a straw and drink

Mash the pulp inside

TIP: EDIBLE DESERT PLANTS

Abal
Acacia
Agave
Baobab
Date palm
Desert amaranth
Wild gourd
Carob
Prickly pear

Prickly pears – liquid can be squeezed from their fruit or lobes.

Saxaul – take the bark and squeeze it to produce water.

Roots – some types of plant, such as the bloodwood desert oak and water tree of Australia, have roots near the surface, and these can be cut and sucked for moisture.

Finding food
Food from animals

Desert insects can be trapped and eaten, but remove the wings and outer shell first before cooking them. Larvae are also edible after cooking.

Larger desert animals that can be trapped and eaten include partridge, quail and bustard, as well as a variety of rodents. Large animals such as antelope or oryx may occasionally appear, but tackle these only if you have appropriate weaponry. When hunting, avoid dangerous insects such as scorpions and steer clear of the wide variety of poisonous snakes and lizards, including the Gila monster and Mexican beaded lizard.

POLAR SURVIVAL

Polar regions are characterized by extreme cold, which can be aggravated by other factors such as wind chill. In polar regions, the sun can remain below the level of the horizon for several months, the only

Windchill factors at an air temperature of 0°C (32°F)	
Wind Speed	**Windchill**
18km/h (11mph)	-9°C (16°F)
35km/h (22mph)	-15°C (5°F)
55km/h (34mph)	-18°C(-0.4°F)
71km/h (44mph)	-20°C (-4°F)

source of warmth being warmer air flowing from southern latitudes. Vegetation is non-existent or sparse. Local animals include the polar bear (Arctic), seals (Arctic and Antarctic) and penguins (Antarctic).

Temperature

Arctic temperatures in the winter can be around -56°C (-81°F), while in the summer, temperatures can climb to 18°C (65°F). In the Antarctic. temperatures can drop to -43°C (-45°F). Another factor is windchill, which can seriously exacerbate the effects of low air temperature.

Clothing

It is essential to have the correct clothing in polar regions. The layering system (see Chapter 4) should be followed and a windproof layer worn as an outer shell. In order to be effective, clothing should be kept as clean and as dry as possible. Do not wear clothing that

Keeping warm

Someone suffering from frostbite or hypothermia should be kept dry and warm with the use of clothing, blankets or a sleeping bag.

is too tight-fitting, as it is important for air to circulate. Wear fur round the hood if possible, as this will help to prevent breath from freezing on your face. Keep the hood and cuffs tightly fastened. These can be loosened if you become too warm when moving or working.

Footwear

There is a wide variety of specialist footwear available for sub-zero conditions. What you wear will depend on the nature of your expedition. Waterproof canvas boots with rubber soles and an insulated liner (known as Mukluks) may be suitable. Wear three layers of socks in your boots. Before entering a shelter or getting into a sleeping bag, try to dust off as much snow as possible.

Water

The amount of clothing worn and the relatively dry air in polar regions means that you can become dehydrated very quickly. Drink regularly and produce a supply of water by melting ice or snow.

During summer months, water should be available from streams, lakes or ponds. In winter, melt ice or snow a little at a time to stop the unmelted snow absorbing melted water back into itself. When looking for ice to melt, choose rounded ice with a bluish tinge, as this will be more palatable.

If you are carrying water in a water bottle, keep it close to your body to reduce the likelihood of it freezing. When filling a water bottle, allow some space in case the water freezes and expands.

Food

The easiest place to find food in polar regions is along the coast, or in streams, rivers and lakes in the summer. Such food might include clams, crawfish, mussels, snails and crabs, as well as a variety of fish and seabirds.

If hunting for seals, beware polar bears that might be hunting the same seal or that may smell the kill. In lower latitudes, animals of the tundra include arctic hares, caribou, lemming, musk ox and reindeer.

Hunting

When hunting, keep the wind in your face and try to keep the sun on your back. If you face into the wind, your scent will be carried away from you and your prey will not be alerted to your presence. Also, your prey will be looking into the sun, which may partially blind them, while you will see them more clearly.

You can build a hide or screen out of snow to observe animals from a sheltered and camouflaged position. When stalking an animal, move very slowly and stop moving entirely whenever an animal raises its head. Keep to soft snow to avoid snow that

Fish basket

A fish trap such as this may take some time and care to construct but will be worth the effort. Form a series of similar length sticks together with a narrow opening; the fish should be able to swim in but not out; place a bait inside.

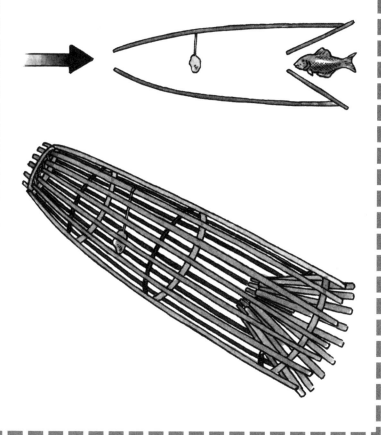

177

crunches noisily underfoot. Do not show yourself above the skyline.

If you have a rifle or catapult, make sure you are within range before attempting to shoot. For large animals, aim behind the ears, behind the foreshoulders or at the throat for the most effective shots.

Polar shelters
It is important to get out of the wind in polar regions. If you need to build a temporary shelter, find a naturally sheltered area that can be adapted, but make sure you are not in an area where a snowdrift or blizzard can bury you.

Snow trench

An effective snow shelter need not be too elaborate. Dig a trench, place snow blocks over it and line the bottom with foliage.

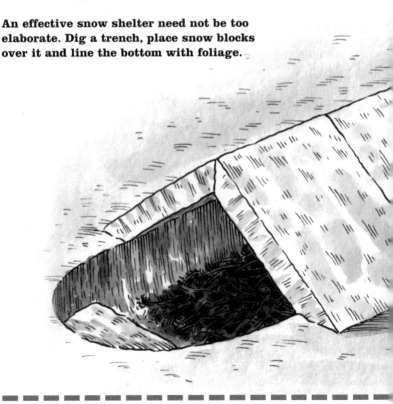

Natural shelters include caves and overhanging rock shelves, spruce trees (dig down to the base of the tree and use the overhanging branches as a natural canopy) or fallen trees with space beneath them.

You can build a range of more elaborate shelters, bearing in mind that these will involve some time and energy. (You may also require tools.) The igloo is the best-known shelter in the polar regions and this requires careful planning and accurate cutting of snow blocks.

A moulded dome shelter is more straightforward to make. This shelter

Pit fire

To keep the fire out of the wind, dig a shallow pit and construct the fire inside it.

involves filling a tarpaulin with bark, twigs and other material to make a ball large enough to create an adequate living space. Cover the ball with snow on a firm surface and allow the snow to solidify. Once it is hard, gradually pull out the contents of the tarpaulin, leaving an interior space. Make sure you always have at least one ventilation hole open in your shelter.

MOUNTAIN SURVIVAL

Conditions encountered in high mountain regions are similar to those found in polar regions, including low temperatures aggravated by a severe windchill factor. Mountainous regions have additional hazards due to steep terrain.

Mountain-climbing and ice-climbing skills are beyond the scope of this book, and if your expedition

TIP: BRAKING POSITION

With an ice axe
Method 1: When sliding on your back, spread your body out and dig in with your heels and ice axe.

Method 2: Place one hand on the head of the axe and the other on the shaft. If your left hand is on the axe head, the adze should be under the left shoulder, with the right hand on the shaft to the side of the body. Push down with the right arm and shoulder so that the pick is forced into the slope. The adze rests in the hollow below the collar bone. Raise your feet and put pressure on the axe and your knees.

Without an ice axe
Roll on your front, push up from the slope with your arms and focus the pressure on your toes. This should create a wedge effect and bring you to a halt. Otherwise, spread your legs and arms to create maximum drag.

takes you to mountainous regions it must be assumed that you have undertaken the necessary training and have the requisite skills. If, however, you find yourself in a mountainous region due to a plane or vehicle accident, your priority is to get down to a lower level as soon as possible in order to find food and shelter. Do not attempt to negotiate mountainous terrain at night, as this is extremely hazardous. You may easily slip and fall over a steep edge.

Glaciers

If you are on or near a glacier, try to cross it in the early morning while it is still cold and before the ice has turned to meltwater. Make sure everyone in your group is roped together, whatever the conditions – fresh snow is likely to cover over crevasses. Allow about 25m (82ft) of rope between two, three or more people. Keep the distance between walkers at about 15m (50ft), and keep the rope taut at all times. If somebody falls into a crevasse, the rest of the team should move quickly backwards and fall back on their haunches to take the strain.

Descent

When you descend down a mountain, kick steps in that snow and use crampons when walking on ice. Make the steps with the heel of the boot, with an almost straight and stiff leg. Hold your ice axe – you

should have one – with the pick pointing backwards and use it for support. Move only when both feet are in the steps.

If you have an ice axe when you slip, drive the shaft into the snow and hold onto it at the base. Kick both your toes into the snow to form a foothold. If it is hard snow, use the sharp pick of the axe to dig into it.

When descending, look out for worn paths or any other signs that the route has been used before. If scrambling down a hillside, face inwards towards the rock, and avoid gullies due to the risk of rock falls.

ABSEILING

To abseil down a mountain side, find a solid anchor and perhaps a backup anchor point for safety. The anchor should preferably be above the ledge on which you are standing. Tie yourself and the top of the abseil rope to the anchor. Tie a knot at the bottom of the abseil rope to avoid abseiling off it. Throw the rope down the cliff. Make sure the rope reaches your destination.

Pass the rope from front to rear between your legs, round your upper left thigh, diagonally across your chest, over your right shoulder, under your armpit and into your left hand. Walk slowly backwards over the edge, crouching if there is any danger the rope may lift off the anchor. Use the lower hand to control the braking, and turn your body outwards and towards the braking hand to see more clearly. Descend as smoothly as possible to avoid a sawing effect on the rope.

Belaying

Belaying is a technique for controlling a climbing rope so that if you fall, you don't drop far. First, cover your arms and wear gloves. Find an anchor, make a loop in the main rope and place it over or round the anchor. Make a figure-of-eight knot to secure it. If necessary, use a back-up anchor. Pass the rope over your head and down to just above the hips. Make a twist round the arm closest to the anchor.

Abseiling

Abseiling can be an effective way of descending safely down a mountainside, but it requires a secure anchor and sufficient rope.

Sit down with your feet firmly anchored. The rope between you and the anchor should be taut. You and the anchor should both be in line with the direction of force. To stop your fall, bring the dead hand across the front of your body. Do not take the dead hand off the rope when the rope is being paid out or drawn in.

Mountain shelters

If it is getting dark, and to avoid moving on a mountain at night, make a shelter on the lee of a boulder or in a natural cave. If there is snow, you

Building a lean-to

A simple lean-to made from branches covered with foliage can provide effective protection from wind and rain.

Building a snow cave

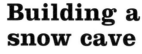

Breathing hole

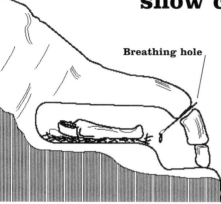

A snow cave can be created by cutting blocks out of a snow drift to create a cavern. Seal the entrance with rucksacks and leave a breathing hole.

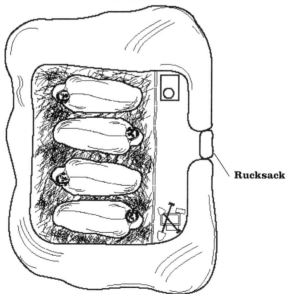

Rucksack

can build a snow cave by cutting into a snow drift and then excavating cavities on either side to create a chamber. You may want to cut out the cavity in blocks. You can use your rucksack to seal the entrance, though you need to have a hole for ventilation.

NAVIGATION

You will need good maps for an expedition, but for certain parts of the world the maps may not be as good as for others. Furthermore, the maps may be lost in a crisis or accident.

It is important to have a reliable compass. Keep your compass amongst your personal equipment or, if you are walking, around your neck on a lanyard. Compasses can be set for different magnetic regions depending on where you are in the world, so make sure that you have the correct code for the region you are visiting.

Taking a bearing

If you are using a plastic compass such as a Silva and you have a map, place your compass on the map with the edge along the direction in which you want to travel. Turn the dial until the 'N' marking north points towards the north in your map and the grid lines in the map are parallel with the lines moulded in the compass dial. You can now read your direction of travel in degrees on the compass.

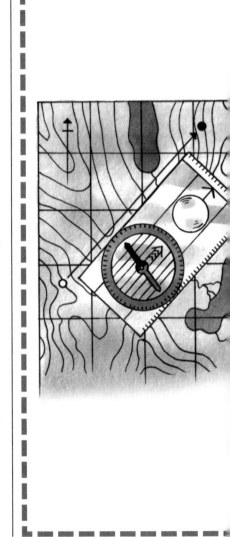

Taking a bearing with compass and map

Effective use of a map and compass will enable you to find a route to safety. Put your compass on the map with the edge along the direction you want to travel. Turn the dial until 'N' points towards the north on your map and the grid lines in the map are parallel with the lines on the compass dial.

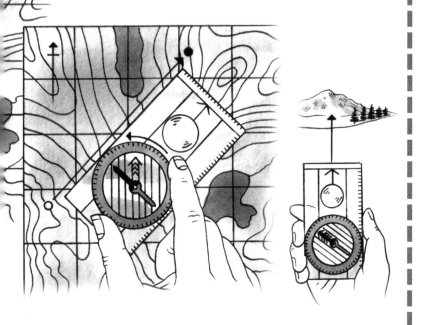

Resection

A resection is a technique for plotting your position by taking bearings on two visible landmarks. It is a useful technique when you are in the middle of a featureless area, such as a plain or desert.

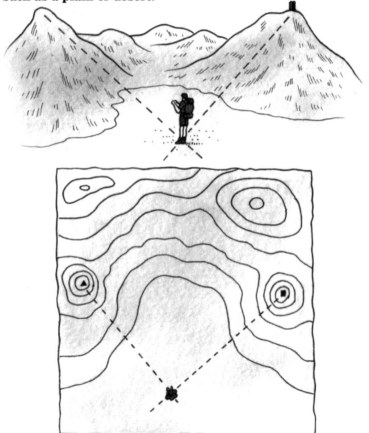

Use your compass to record the bearing of two landmarks, then plot the bearing on your map.

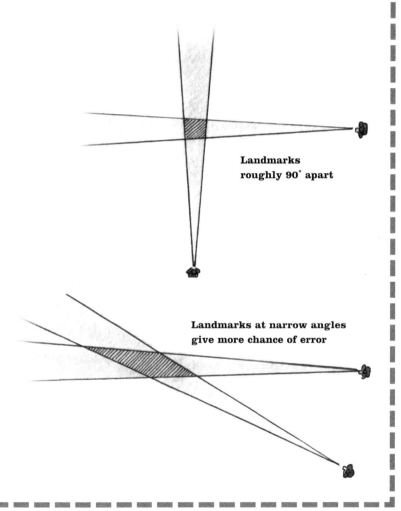

Landmarks roughly 90° apart

Landmarks at narrow angles give more chance of error

MAGNETIC REGION CODES

MN   – magnetic northern
        hemisphere
NME   – north magnetic
        equatorial region
SME   – south magnetic
        equatorial region
MS   – magnetic southern
        hemisphere

In order to follow the compass in the direction you wish to travel, take the compass off the map and align the magnetic needle with the marked arrow showing 'N' in the compass bezel. The compass is now pointing in the direction you wish to travel.

In order not to come off route, set your sights on a landmark that is in line with the compass direction. Once you have reached the landmark, set your sights on another, and so on until you reach your destination. Take into account the possibility that you may lose sight of the landmark if you go down hill or enter a wood.

Compass bearings

If you have a map, it should show the difference between geographic north and magnetic north. This difference is known as declination. If you have an easterly declination, use the declination scale inside the capsule of your compass until it points to 20° on the declination scale. The direction of travel arrow is now pointing in the direction of travel.

Pacing

When soldiers are taught navigation, they are also taught to measure their pacing. The best way to measure your pacing is against a known distance before you set out on an expedition. Measure a full pace each time your right heel hits the ground and record how many paces you make in the measured distance:

- On the flat
- With a load
- On hilly ground

If you have a pedometer, make sure you know how to use it and that it is adjusted to your individual pace. By using pacing, you can obtain a much more accurate fix on your position as you progress towards your destination.

Navigating with the sun

If you do not have a map or compass, you can use the sun to orientate yourself by studying its position. Remember that the sun rises in the east and sets in the west. If you are north of the Tropic of Cancer, the position of the sun at midday will be south. If you are south of the Tropic of Capricorn, the position of the sun at midday will be north.

Using an analogue watch

Take an accurate and reliable analogue watch on your expedition. Using the watch face, and at nine o'clock in the morning in the northern hemisphere, point the hour hand at the sun. The bisected angle between the hour hand and the minute hand will indicate south and north (see diagram page 294).

In the southern hemisphere, do the same but with 12 pointed towards the sun. North will be midway between the hour hand and 12 o'clock.

Sun-shadow method

Place a stick about 1m (3ft) high in the ground. Make sure that the ground around the stick is as flat as possible. Mark the tip of the shadow of the stick on the ground. Wait about 15 minutes and then mark the tip of the shadow again. Make a line between the two points you have marked. This gives a rough indication of the east–west line. If you then bisect this line, you will also get the north-south line.

Star navigation

In the northern hemisphere, use Polaris (the North Star) as the best indication of north. Polaris occurs in the constellation Ursa Minor (Little Bear). You can also use the

MAGNETIC VARIATION

'Magnetic variation' (MVAR) is the difference between true north and magnetic north.

If the MVAR is west, you add it to a true bearing to obtain a magnetic bearing.

If the MVAR is east, you subtract it from a true bearing to get a magnetic bearing.

GRID MAGNETIC ANGLE (GMA)

The GMA is the angular difference in direction between grid north and magnetic north. It is measured east or west from grid north.

If the GMA is west, you add it to the grid bearing to obtain a magnetic bearing.

If the GMA is east, you subtract it from a grid bearing to obtain a magnetic bearing.

Navigating with a watch

In the northern hemisphere, point the hour hand at the sun and bisect the angle between it and 12 o'clock to find south. In the southern hemisphere, point the 12 o'clock mark at the sun and bisect the angle between the mark and the hour hand to find north.

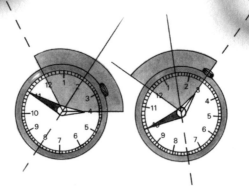

constellations Ursa Major (Great Bear), Orion and Cassiopeia to help locate Polaris (see diagram pages 296–297). By calculating the vertical angle to Polaris, you can work out your latitude. Note that as you move further south, Polaris will appear lower in the sky.

Although there is a star near the South Pole, it is too faint to use as an accurate navigational reference. In order to find south, use the Southern Cross constellation as well as the bright star in the Hydrus constellation – B Hydrus. Draw a line between B Hydrus and the Southern Cross and then extend the longer axis 4.5 times to mark a point that will be directly above geographic south.

Direction by shadow

Casting a shadow using a stick embedded in the ground can provide you with direction imformation, using time-elapse plotting. A line joining the tips of two consecutively marked shadows runs approximately east–west. Another line marked at a 90 degree angle will give you the north–south coordinates.

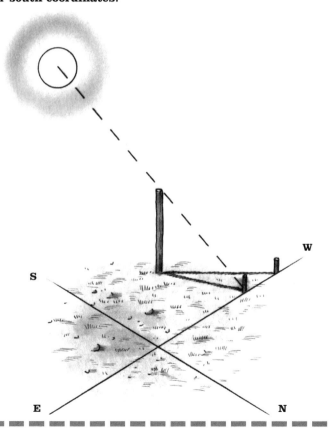

North Star

The Pole Star, North Star or Polaris (to use its three most popular names) is a sure indicator of north. Extending lines out from the Big Dipper (Plough) or from Cassiopeia as shown will help you correctly identify the North Star, which sits in a relatively isolated aspect in the night sky.

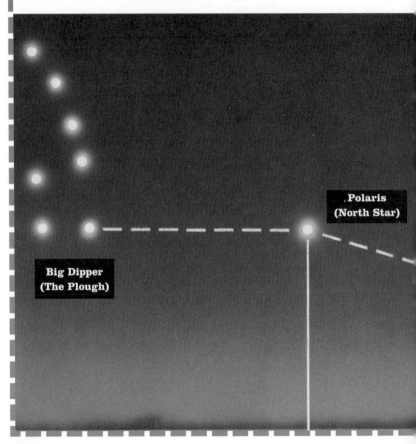

Polaris (North Star)

Big Dipper (The Plough)

Cassiopeia

TIP: STAR MOVEMENTS

You can orientate yourself by star movements:

Northern Hemisphere
- Star rising – it is in the east
- Star falling – it is in the west
- Star moving left – it is in the north
- Star moving right – it is in the south

Southern hemisphere
- Star rising – it is in the west
- Star falling – it is in the east
- Star moving left – it is in the south
- Star moving right – it is in the north

RESCUE

The priority in a crisis is to signal for help. This priority overrides almost every other plan, apart from first aid requirements and finding essential water and shelter (especially in desert or polar conditions).

Building a signal fire

To maintain a signal fire in snowy or wet conditions, provide a solid base with logs underneath.

The internationally recognized distress signals are SOS and Mayday (for radio signals). You can also signal distress by sounding signals in groups of three or providing visual signals in groups of three (such as three columns of smoke from fires). When signalling with a noise (such as gunfire), wait for a minute between each report.

There are other signals that are recognized in certain areas. For example, the International Mountain Distress Signal is six whistles per minute, followed by a minute's silence. Repeat continually. You can send the same signal using a flashlight.

Plan your signalling strategy so that you place visual signals in areas where they are most likely to be seen (for example, in a clearing or on the top of a ridge). Prepare signals so that they are ready to be used at the most opportune moment – for example, when the sound of an aircraft is heard in the distance. Burn green foliage to make maximum smoke. In polar regions, burn rubber if available.

If you have a survival tin, you can use the inside of the tin or a mirror to flash SOS signals to passing search parties, aircraft or ships, depending on your location. The Morse Code for SOS is three short, three long, three short.

Body signals

Body signals can be used to communicate with rescue aircraft.

Affirmative (yes)

Our receiver is operating

Do not land here

Pick us up

Ground to air signals

1

Another way of communicating with aircraft is through ground-to-air signals, using stones, logs or marks on the ground.

2

1. Need doctor—serious injuries
2. Need medical supplies
3. Unable to proceed
4. Need food and water
5. Need firearms and ammunition
6. Need map and compass
7. Need signal lamp with battery and radio
8. Indicate direction to proceed
9. Am proceeding in this direction
10. Will attempt take-off
11. Aircraft seriously damaged
12. Probably safe to land here
13. Need food and oil
14. All well
15. No
16. Yes
17. Not understood
18. Need engineer

3

4

5

6

7

13

8

14

9

15

10

16

11

17

12

18

Using a strop

A helicopter rescue strop should be placed securely under the arms. Do not lift your arms above your chest when being lifted.

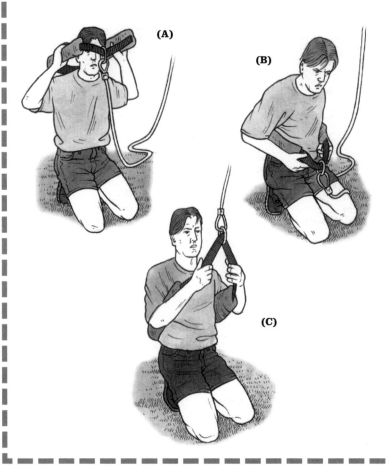

(A)

(B)

(C)

(D)

Rescue by helicopter

A helicopter is the most likely means used if you are to be evacuated by air search-and-rescue teams. Make sure you get into a clear area that is free from obstructions and not too close to trees or any other hazards.

If a helicopter lands, do not approach it until signalled to do so by the crew. Do not approach the helicopter from the rear because you will be in danger from the rear rotor. Keep well below the level of the main rotor blades and do not lift anything or anyone above your head (such as carrying a child on your shoulders).

If the helicopter remains hovering and lowers a winchman, do exactly what he says as calmly as possible. Should the helicopter lower a strop, place it over your head and arms and under your armpits. If there is an adjustment ring, slide it down towards your chest to tighten it. When you are ready, do a thumbs-up signal to the winchman. Keep your arms folded over your chest or by your side – do not reach up to the cable above you. Remain in this position until you reach the helicopter. Do not attempt to remove the strop until you are told to do so.

There is a vast selection of good quality outdoor clothing and equipment available both on the high street and online. The only real problem you will have before setting off on an expedition is choosing between many equally good brands. It is highly recommended that you take time to get some good advice from a well-trained shop assistant in a well-known outdoor outlet. Beware of walking into larger outlets on the weekend, where you may find a part-time shop assistant who will tell you whatever you want to hear. A careful choice at this stage will save you a lot of time, money and pain in the future.

BOOTS

Boots are probably the personal clothing item you will want to spend most time getting right. They may look good and be well designed for the job in hand, but if your new boots are not the right fit for your feet you may be almost crippled by blisters and other foot injuries and become a burden to the rest of your team.

The first, most obvious question is how will you use your boots? What part of the world are you visiting and what kind of terrain will you be walking over?

....

Left: **Having the right kit and equipment could save your life in a crisis situation.**

5

Having the right equipment will vastly improve your chances of survival in a crisis.

Preparation

Kit and Equipment

A typical profile for walking will be something like this:
- Mountain walking
- Hill walking
- Fell walking
- Paths/trails

If you are likely to be walking on snow and ice, you will obviously need crampons – your boot will need to be stiff enough to attach these. If you are mostly going to be walking on fells and hills, you will not want a fully

Walking equipment

It is worth taking time to select the right equipment for your expedition so that you are both comfortable and well prepared.

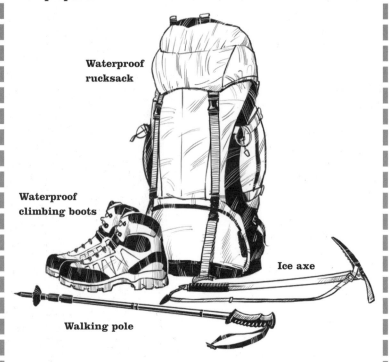

Waterproof rucksack

Waterproof climbing boots

Ice axe

Walking pole

stiffened mountain boot. Depending on your activities and plans, you may need more than one pair of boots.

If you are a serious mountain climber, you can choose specialist boots within that category and some that will cover all the categories, including:

- Sport
- Bouldering
- Indoor
- Trad
- Multi-pitch

Apart from the terrain, you also need to consider what kind of load you will be carrying, as this will have an impact on the stiffness level and support of the boot.

Boots are broadly divided into fabric-and-leather and all-leather. Which you should choose is partly a matter of taste. Suede-type leathers need to be maintained with protective sprays, so if you prefer using grease and polish you may want to opt for traditional full-grain smooth leather boots. It may be an advantage to have fully waterproof boots. Apart from Gore-Tex®, there are now a number of high-specification waterproof fabrics and liners that provide protection from water.

In order to test the correct fit for a boot, you need to wear the kind of socks (i.e. walking socks, perhaps with liners) that you will be wearing outdoors. It helps to try boots on in

TIP: LACING HELPS

Once you have chosen the right kind of boots for your activity, you can also lace the boots in different ways to suit your walking style and the shape of your foot.

- If you feel pressure from the laces on the upper part of your foot, try missing out the set of eyelets in that area and move on to the next set. This will leave a space in the pressure area.
- If the knot is uncomfortable against your upper ankle, lace up to the top eyelets and then down again to tie the knot lower down.
- If the lacing tends to loosen in the lower area of the boot, try tying a knot further down before carrying on with the lacing and tying another knot at the top.
- If the ends of the laces are flapping around, tie a triple or quadruple knot to use up the free ends.

TIP: WHAT KIND OF BOOT?

- To get an idea what kind of boot you are trying, pinch the toe box on both sides. If the toe box gives way relatively easily under pressure, this boot will be for country trails and lower level walking. If the toe box is rigid, it is likely to be a mountain and winter boot.
- You can do the same with the heel counter. Bend the toe of the boot back towards the heel. If it is easily flexible, this is a boot for low-level walking. If it is stiff, this is a mountain/winter boot.
- Note that when leather gets wet, it looses some of its waterproof qualities and becomes less pliable.
- Make sure you feed leather regularly with the recommended treatments.

the afternoon when your feet are warmer and have expanded a little.

When selecting the right kind of boots, make sure that they are not too wide. A good way to test this is by standing on an incline (they may have one in the shop) to test whether your feet slide forward in the boot. If they do, try another pair – you may need to try another brand of boot altogether. Bear in mind that northern Europeans tend to have wider feet than southern Europeans. So, if you have a narrow foot, you may find that an Italian brand, for example, suits you best. The height of the arch in the boot may also influence foot movement. Some boots are relatively flat internally whereas others are sculpted, with a high arch. It will depend on the shape of your feet (i.e. the depth of arch in your foot) as to which will be most comfortable. If the boot suits you in other respects, such as width, but you want a higher arch, take a look at the available insoles. These can often be bought separately in good retailers and may solve your problem.

Remember, when you buy boots (or running shoes, for that matter) the size will not be the same size as the shoes you use for everyday. You need to allow extra space for foot movement and bulkier socks. When you 'run in' your boots, take it in easy stages so that the boot has time to adapt to your individual foot shape and bed into the insole.

CLOTHING

Layering

The layering system has now become familiar to many people. The principle is used by NATO and other armed forces and is also used for leisure wear. The British Army Combat 95 clothing system, for example, uses technology that has been learned from the leisure and sport industries.

Base layer

This should be a light, perhaps synthetic, material that can wick away perspiration to the outer layers. Although cotton is still sometimes used as a base layer, it has a tendency to retain moisture and needs to be removed if it becomes too wet. A synthetic fibre base layer will wick moisture away from the skin towards the outer layers. The type of base layer you choose will also depend on the temperature zone you are entering.

Mid-layer

You can wear a standard-style shirt (either cotton or synthetic). The British armed forces and the Royal Netherlands Army are issued a Norwegian-style shirt, which is a loose-fitting long-sleeve shirt with a zip collar for temperature control. Most NATO military forces use a fleece or Polartec®-type synthetic bodywarmer with a high insulating capacity. This normally has a front zip fastener and a roll collar. Sometimes fleeces also feature underarm zips for further temperature control. Military and civilian versions may have arm patches for greater durability. If the weather is relatively mild and dry, the fleece can be used as the outer layer. The fleece issued to the Canadian Army is made from polyester with double-sided velour pile. Fleeces have replaced the ribbed woollen sweaters in the British armed forces, though wool sweaters still provide good mid-layer insulation. Wool fibres hold their own micro-climate and they do not absorb very much water.

Outer layer

This is sometimes known as the shell, and it is normally both windproof and waterproof. Ideally the fabric should be breathable. The choice of outer garment will depend on the weather zone you are visiting and also the terrain. For mountain climbing, you may need a very heavy-duty outer shell such as a parka. Otherwise, there are some excellent products on the market for all round hill walking. Sometimes outer shells are provided with zips so that you can incorporate a mid-layer fleece for colder conditions.

Trousers and leg warmers

Similar rules cover trousers and leg warmers as your other layers. You can wear an inner wicking layer of underwear beneath your trousers.

Waterproof clothing

Keeping both dry and warm is essential when outdoors for long periods.

Thermal gloves

Waterproof jacket

Waterproof leggings

For trekking, trousers should be relatively loose fitting and made from a hard-wearing material. Norwegian Army trousers are made from water-repellent cotton sateen, while the Danish Army is issued with trousers that are made from cotton/polyamide with a rip-stop twill fabric. Similar civilian trousers, with zip and map pockets, can be bought at reasonable prices on the high street and online. Apart from the loose fit, these trousers are designed to absorb minimum moisture.

It is useful to carry a pair of waterproof and breathable

Cold climate dress

The layering system enables you to adapt your clothing according to the temperature and the level of physical activity.

overtrousers. Keep these in the top of your backpack for when the weather gets wet and windy.

Hat, gloves and socks

Although most good-quality outer coats will be equipped with a packaway hood, a good hat can be more comfortable and convenient to wear for general use. Some hats are easily folded to pack away in a jacket pocket or in the top of a rucksack.

The type of gloves you choose will depend on the environment. You may need two pairs – one without a liner for dexterous work and another thicker pair for colder weather.

Socks are often referred to as 'sock systems' due to the fact that they may incorporate a pair of liner

TIP: DRYING YOUR BOOTS

- Clean your boots thoroughly with water if they are muddy.
- Dry the boots by stuffing them with newspaper and leaving them in a warm environment (not too near to the heat source).
- Once they are dry, re-proof them with a recommended treatment.

ESSENTIAL KIT LIST

- Tent
- Sleeping bag
- Sleeping mat
- Mosquito net
- Hammock
- Towel
- Flashlight (plus spare batteries)
- Digging spade
- Knife and / or multi-tool
- First aid kit
- Survival tin
- Water bottles – preferably aluminium, but you can use plastic if it is tough and will not crack.
- Mess tin – or something similar. Mess tins are used by the British Army, who pack other essentials such as wash kit inside them.
- Wash kit – carry only as much as you need.
- Compass – either the Silva compass or a prismatic sighting compass. The genuine prismatic compasses can be very expensive, but there are some good, cheaper varieties available.
- Map case – this will keep your map dry and the clear plastic ones will

allow you to read the map on the move.
- Walking pole or stick – these can be aluminium and telescopic or you can use a traditional wooden one.

- Ice pick – essential for movements above the snow line and on mountains.
- Rope (walking and/or climbing)
- Climbing harness
- Spare carabiners

Learning to use a compass correctly will greatly increase your chances of surviving a crisis.

Steering compass

Baseplate compass with sighting mirror and clinometer

Prismatic compass

socks, designed to wick perspiration away from the foot, and a thicker pair of woollen socks designed to keep the feet warm and provide good contact with the boot. Plan the kind of sock system you will use before buying your boots, as a bulky sock system will need plenty of room in the boot. Do not wear a sock system on trust or recommendation alone. Try it out to test whether it gives you blisters or not.

BACKPACK

If you are embarking on an expedition, you will obviously need to choose a backpack that suits. You may find that the type of backpack will mirror the type of boots you wear.

Once you have selected a backpack according to use (e.g. hill walking or mountain climbing) and the amount of equipment you need to carry, you will be faced with a number of competing brands. As with boots, it will be worth taking advice from an experienced store specialist to get this right.

A backpack may come in different sizes within a particular range, so you will need to measure your torso from the top of your hips to the base of your neck to work out what size it should be. Some backpacks have adjustable systems, so you can fit the pack at home.

When choosing a backpack, think carefully about the weight distribution. Modern backpacks are usually designed with effective hip belts that help to distribute the weight around the hips and take the strain off the shoulders. Different brands have different technologies, so it may take time to find the one that suits you best.

Packing your backpack

Pack your clothing into waterproof tough plastic bags and pack them in the backpack according to how soon you will need the items – sleeping garments, for example, will go near the bottom whereas spare socks will go near the top where they are accessible. This will keep essential clothing dry. Pack heavier equipment and stores towards the inner part of the backpack, but keep something soft between your back and anything hard. Also keep heavier stores low in the backpack, so that the weight does not cause destabilization at the top.

GAITERS

These are an excellent piece of additional equipment, as they protect the lower legs from wet undergrowth as well as thorns, mud and snow.

SURVIVAL TIN

Special forces soldiers carry a survival tin in their personal webbing system (not in the Bergen backpack). This means that in an emergency they can dump their heavy loads and still have some essential tools of survival.

Survival tin contents

- Commando wire saw (with rings that act as finger pulls)
- Penknife (if it is rather blunt, either sharpen or replace with a better penknife, such as the Spyderco Ladybug)
- Flint and steel striker (saw-blade type)
- Razor blade

Survival tin

A survival tin contains essential items for making shelter, catching food and purifying water in extreme circumstances.

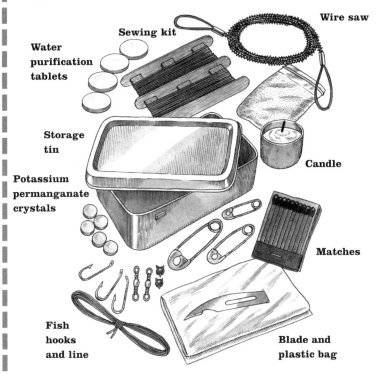

Water purification tablets

Sewing kit

Wire saw

Storage tin

Candle

Potassium permanganate crystals

Matches

Fish hooks and line

Blade and plastic bag

- Small stub candle
- Button compass (a brass button is best, but plastic will suffice)
- Brass snare wire
- Fishing line
- Fish hooks
- Fishing weights
- Fishing swivel
- Waterproof matches
- Water purification tables (chlorine based)
- Candle
- Whistle
- Safety pins
- Pencil
- Sewing kit
- Potassium permanganate crystals
- Insulating tape (for wrapping around outside of tin to make it watertight)
- Condom – for carrying water
- Tampon – great tinder for taking

Types of fish hooks

You can adapt your survival tin by taking a variety of hooks, weights and lures for fishing.

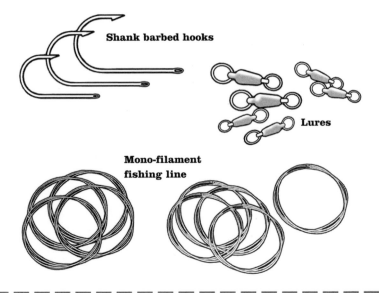

Shank barbed hooks

Lures

Mono-filament fishing line

a spark when firelighting, as well as the intended use.
- Adhesive plasters
- Waterproof survival instructions
- Storage tin (tin lid serves as signalling mirror)

Tent

As with all equipment discussed in this section, you will be spoilt for choice with tents. The main criteria on which you should aim to choose a tent are:

Size: is it just for yourself or do you need a 2-, 3- or 4-person tent for companions? If you just need one for yourself, you might want to consider taking a two-man tent, which will provide extra space for storage, as long as you are prepared to carry the extra weight.

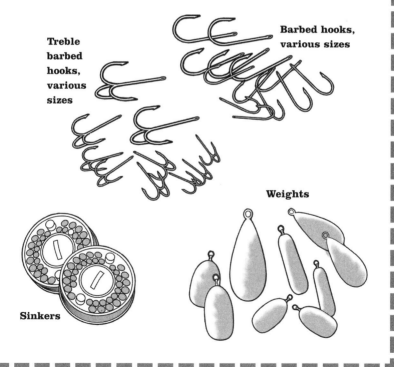

Treble barbed hooks, various sizes

Barbed hooks, various sizes

Weights

Sinkers

FIRST AID KIT

Single person
- Non-adherent dressing 5 x 5cm (2 x 2in)
- 4 sterile wound dressings
- Pkt 12 assorted safety pins
- Pair of vinyl gloves
- 6 alcohol-free antiseptic wipes
- Micropore tape 1.25cm x 10m (0.5in x 33ft)
- Waterproof dressing strip 4 x 1cm (1.5 x 0.4in)
- Bandage 7.5cm x 5m (3 x 2in) BP quality
- Resuscitator
- Plastic tweezers
- Non-woven triangular bandage
- 2 steri-strip 7.5 x 3cm (3 x 1.2in) – strip of 5
- 50g (1.7oz) antiseptic

Gregson Pack NATO approved first aid kit
- Tweezers
- Antiseptic wipes
- Adhesive dressings
- Isolaide resuscitator
- Dumbell sutures (x5)
- No 3 dressing
- No 8 dressing
- Paratulle
- No 16 dressing

- Triangular bandage
- Anchor dressing
- Wow bandage
- Zinc oxide plaster roll
- Crepe bandage
- Orange drink sachet

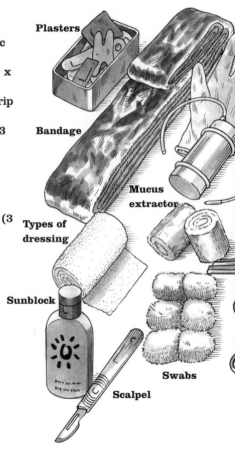

Plasters

Bandage

Mucus extractor

Types of dressing

Sunblock

Swabs

Scalpel

- Large disposable gloves
- Strip fabric dressing
- Safety pins (x6)
- Folding scissors
- 12.7cm (5in) scissors
- Microporous adhesive tape
- Peha crepe bandage
- Accident evaluation report
- First aid hints booklet
- Contents leaflet
- Car sticker

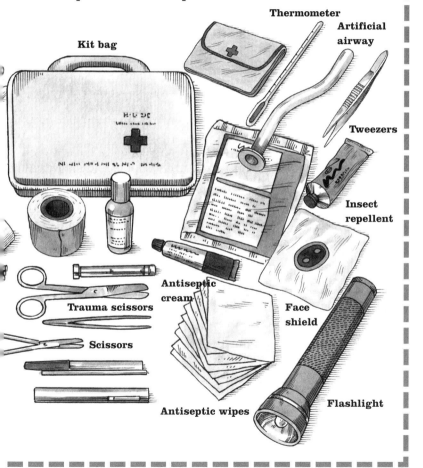

Thermometer

Artificial airway

Kit bag

Tweezers

Insect repellent

Trauma scissors

Antiseptic cream

Face shield

Scissors

Antiseptic wipes

Flashlight

Types of tent

Choose a tent according to the amount of space you need and also the terrain and weather conditions.

Tunnel

Geodesic

Dome

Design: there are a variety of tent designs on the market and individual manufacturers are always seeking to make improvements both in design and in materials.

• *Tunnel:* this design tends to be less heavy and the tent is comparatively spacious.
• *Geodesic:* this design incorporates crossed poles, which makes the tent very stable. Geodesic tents are ideal for severe weather and exposed conditions.
• *Dome:* this design is used where maximum space is a priority. The dome tents are not as stable as the geodesic designs and therefore should only be used in less exposed conditions.

Apart from the type of tent, which will be suited to the individual requirements of your expedition, you will also want to check:

Height: in a small tent, you will obviously not expect to be able to stand, but you will want enough headroom to sit up comfortably without touching the ceiling with your head.

Length: is the sleeping compartment long enough for you to lie down comfortably with a little room to spare? If you are more than 1.8m (6ft) tall, you will want to double-check that the length is adequate. A reasonable length for a three-man tent will be 2.05m (6ft 8in).

Width: check there is enough width for the number of people, taking into account extra space for equipment and movement. For three people, a width of 2m (6ft 7in) is adequate.

Storage: in addition to the living/sleeping space, you will probably want an outer storage area to store a backpack, boots and other equipment. Sometimes this storage area will have a groundsheet.

Layers: does the tent have an inner and outer layer? Two layers offers better protection from the elements.

The quality of the tent and the price tag will partly depend on the materials used. Poles may be fibreglass, aluminium or alloy. The outer material will probably be a rip-stop PU-coated polyester, the toughness of which will depend on the conditions for which it was designed. Do not buy a tent designed for pitching next to a car or by a beach if you want to do rough camping on windy hills. You can also buy 'quick-pitch' tents which, as their name suggests, are designed to be extremely easy to erect – making them handy in a rainstorm.

W hether you are planning to go on a specific expedition or not, having a healthy body and keeping fit will always be an advantage in a crisis. Much of the stress of everyday, urban life is due to the fact that there is little physical outlet for stress. The modern person may start the day with a commute to work amongst traffic or crowds of people. He will sit in an office all day. When he returns home after again sitting in traffic or standing in a crowded train, he may 'relax' by watching television.

None of this activity provides the opportunity to burn away stress through regular physical exercise. As a result, there is considerable strain on the body's systems. If no exercise is taken at all over a long period, muscles weaken or atrophy, the body stores more fat, heart rate speeds up and blood pressure rises.

To stay fit, you need to maintain a regular programme of exercise. The body responds to the requirements placed upon it. If there are no requirements, it will simply return to its unfit state. Your fitness levels are in proportion to the amount of time and effort you put into it. If you stop training altogether, you will maintain

....

Left: A regular exercise routine will help you to develop physical and mental endurance, enhancing your ability to cope with crisis.

6

A fit and healthy body is a key to survival in crisis situations.

Preparation

Healthy Body

Diet

A well-planned diet will improve your health and sense of wellbeing. It will enhance physical and mental functions. You should aim for a balance of protein, carbohydrates and vitamin-rich foods such as fruit and vegetables.

TIP:
BENEFITS OF FITNESS

A healthy fitness regime, involving regular running and / or another cardiovascular exercise, will have numerous positive effects on the body:

- Bones thicken in the feet and legs and become more robust
- Heart walls thicken and heart chambers enlarge
- Joints become lubricated and work more efficiently
- Muscles in the diaphragm become stronger and more efficient, making breathing easier
- The number of blood vessels feeding each muscle cell increases
- Mitochondria are multiplied, which enhances the ability of muscle cells to use oxygen more efficiently to produce energy
- The rate at which muscle cells burn fat to produce energy is increased
- Fast-twitch muscles in the body increase resistance to fatigue
- During exercise, the respiratory system is cleared of mucus, making breathing more efficient
- The skin becomes more efficient in regulating heat and resisting cold
- Perspiration resulting from intensive exercise cleanses the skin pores and reduces the likelihood of catching skin-related infections.

the level of fitness at which you stopped for about a week. There may even be a benefit in the break from training, as the body regains some of the strength it may have lost from a tiring training regime. If the training stops for any longer than that, however, your body will quickly revert to its previous condition. Beyond the first week, your muscles begin to lose their aerobic capacity – this can reduce by between 10 and 50 per cent, depending on your lifestyle. The capillaries that feed the muscle fibres will decrease by a similar percentage. The result of this is that less oxygen is carried to the muscle fibres and that waste products are removed less

Muscle health

Regular muscle training improves posture and provides an excellent platform for sports and activities.

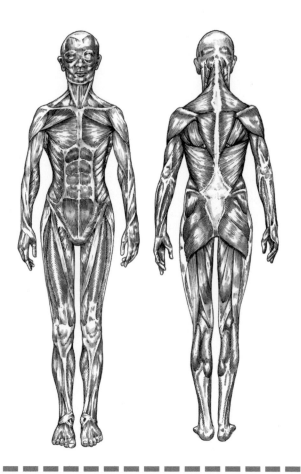

Resting heart rate

Check your resting heart rate to assess your current fitness level.

efficiently. After a period of about a month, even an athlete may be at the same level in these areas as an average, unfit individual.

The good news is that your body adapts relatively quickly to the demands placed upon it. Keeping fit is a life choice that will make you feel better, and probably help you to live longer. In order to gauge how fit you are and what kind of fitness programme you need to start, it is a good idea first to carry out a health check.

HEALTH CHECK

A health check is an inventory of your physical state, and it ranges from measuring your heart rate to analyzing how much you eat and drink and how sedentary or active you are.

Resting heart rate

Measuring your resting heart rate (RHR) is one of the best ways of assessing your fitness. In order for the measurement to be as accurate as possible, it is best to measure your RHR when you are completely still, preferably first thing in the morning. Stimulants such as caffeine in coffee or tea will affect your heart rate, so try to measure it before you have taken any of these drinks. Medicines may also affect your RHR and you should not attempt to assess your RHR when you are ill. Smoking will alter your RHR – if you plan to get fit and stay fit, you will need to permanently give up smoking anyway (smoking also has a significant effect on lung function) – as will an over-active thyroid. In order to get the most accurate reading, you should take the RHR on three separate occasions and then work out the average.

There are different ways of measuring your RHR, the simplest being to put two fingers against the artery on the side of your neck and count the beats for a timed full minute (or alternatively, count the beats for 10 seconds and then

Strength training

Strength training with weights at least two days every week is an important part of your fitness regime.

multiply the score by six). Another way of measuring your RHR is by using a heart rate monitor, which can be purchased at a sports outlet. These come in either wristwatch form or they can be strapped to the chest.

If you are a man in your mid to late thirties, an average RHR may be 71–75 beats per minute (BPM). Below average might be 76–82 BPM.

Excellent might be 57–62 BPM. If you have a RHR of 50–56 BPM, congratulations: you are probably slated to take part in the next Olympic Games! If you are a woman, take into account the fact that women's hearts tend to beat about five BPM faster than men's.

The higher your RHR, the more work you need to do to get fit and bring it down. You will not get fit overnight, however, so do not strain yourself in your enthusiasm to become fit and well. Your body will immediately adjust to a training regime, but you will strain yourself if you push yourself too hard at first.

Training heart rate

The training heart rate (THR) will provide an indication of how your heart reacts when exerted. It is the rate at which your heart beats to provide optimum cardiovascular training and conditioning. This rate will be between 70 and 80 per cent of your maximum heart rate.

If you train too far below this figure, you will not be improving your cardiovascular fitness. If you train too far above it, you will risk strain or injury. One way of estimating your

TIP:
AEROBIC EXERCISE AND STRENGTH-TRAINING WEEKLY REGIME

The American College of Sports Medicine (ACSM) says that a well-rounded physical exercise programme should include both aerobic and strength-training exercise, though not necessarily in the same session. Such a programme should maintain or improve cardio-respiratory and muscular fitness as well as overall health and body function.

Aerobic exercises include walking, running, stair climbing, cycling, rowing, swimming and cross-country skiing. The ACSM physical activity recommendations can be summarized as:

- At least 30 minutes of moderate-intensity physical activity (hard enough to produce perspiration, but allowing conversation) five days per week, or...
- 20 minutes of more vigorous activity three days per week, or...
- A combination of the above.
- Strength training should be performed a minimum of two days each week, and include 8–12 different exercises targeting all major muscle groups.

THR is by subtracting your age from 220 and calculating 70 and 80 per cent of the figure you get. You can also measure your THR by feeling your pulse for 10 seconds after exercise and multiplying by six, or holding it for a whole minute, or by using a heart rate monitor.

Maximum heart rate

Maximum heart rate (MHR) occurs when your heart can no longer provide more oxygen because it cannot beat any faster. You can measure your MHR by subtracting your age from 220 or by running hard for three minutes in two sessions and measuring your pulse after each run.

Have a relaxed jog both between sessions and afterwards. Because you are pushing your heart rate literally to its limit, it is important that you carry out the physical version of this test only when you are fully fit and also warmed up.

There are a variety of other ways in which you can assess your level of fitness:

- You can test your blood pressure. This can be done with equipment you can purchase yourself or by a health professional at a clinic. Bear in mind that, like your RHR, your blood pressure level can be affected by a variety of factors, including stress. Sometimes the anxiety of measuring your blood pressure is enough to raise it.

- You can test the size and efficiency of your lungs by using specialist equipment (a peak flow meter), which will probably be available from a clinic, health or sports club.

- You can measure your body fat percentage either in a rudimentary way (by seeing how much skin you can pinch around your waist) or by using body callipers.

- You can test your flexibility by attempting to touch your toes with your fingers without bending your legs (remember, do not bounce on the stretch). At this point, you are just assessing your baseline fitness, so do not overdo it.

- Test your upper-body strength by seeing how many press-ups you can do. If you can do only one, that is fine. Even that attempt will have slightly strengthened your body so that next time you can do it better. The body always adapts to training, but it just needs reasonable time for change.

- To test your abdominal strength, try some sit-ups. Put your hands near your ears, lie flat on your back, bend your legs so that your feet are flat on the floor and try to raise your body about 30° from the ground. Lie back and repeat for as many times as you can. You may need a counterweight on your feet.

Aerobic training

Aerobic exercise such as rowing is performed at a moderate level of intensity over an extended period of time. This will improve your endurance and fitness.

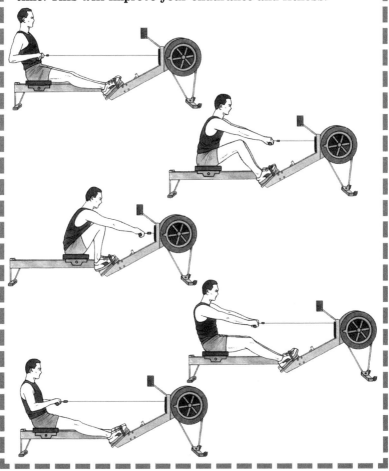

Warming the muscles

A regular routine of stretching and warm-ups should accompany any exercise programme. Seated leg pushes are a good way of warming the core of your body.

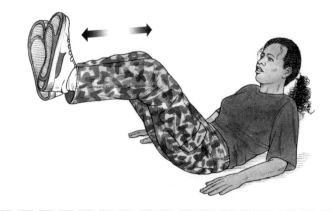

TIP:
SKIPPING

Although mostly associated with young girls, skipping is a good exercise at any age to supplement your fitness regime. You can skip either in a step-through motion or by jumping with both feet together. Apart from improving your overall fitness, skipping also improves balance and coordination. It may take some practice to get it right, or take some advice from your local school!

Lunges

Simple exercises with dumbbells can help to strengthen and give more power to your legs. Place one leg forwards, and one leg back, bending at the knees. Jump up and reverse your legs as you do. Repeat 10 times.

WARM-UP AND COOL-DOWN

Before you do any physical exercise, and especially if you are unfit, have not exercised for a long time or have any kind of stiffness in your limbs, make sure that you go through a regular warm-up routine. A cool-down is less important in my view, but it be helpful if your exercise routine has been very intensive or involved resistance training such as weights or cycling.

The point of the warm-up and cool-down is to reduce the tension in muscles in order to allow you to take exercise more efficiently. Stretching exercises literally enable the muscles to stretch further. This extra capacity helps you to lengthen your stride and have more efficient and comfortable body movements overall. The more a muscle is stretched (within reasonable limits), the more efficiently it will perform.

Any time spent stretching can be helpful. Before an intensive session of activity, athletes tend to warm-up for between 10 and 15 minutes. It is

TIP:
WARMING-UP AND COOLING-DOWN
ROUTINES

Warming up and cooling down helps to improve the flow of blood around the body, improves muscle efficiency and helps to make muscles and ligaments more elastic.
A typical warm-up might include:

- 15-minute jog;
- 5 minutes gentle stretching.

When stretching, pay particular attention to the muscle groups that are relevant to your sport. For example, a swimmer may concentrate more on the upper body, including arms and shoulders, while a runner may focus on legs and torso.

A cool-down helps the body to get rid of the waste products that may have built up during exercise. The cool-down may include a similar short jog and some gentle stretching.

even more important to warm-up and stretch if you have recently been doing strenuous exercise or if the weather is cold.

Remember, though, that incorrect stretching can be a cause of injury in itself. Common mistakes are over-enthusiastic stretching, when a muscle is stretched too far before it is properly warmed up, and 'bouncing' on a stretch. Both can rapidly push to the limit of muscle stretch and cause muscle strain.

When you reach the limit of your stretch – when the muscle is tight and you feel a little pain – hold it gently at that point for a few moments and then release the strain. When you go back carefully to the same point again, you will probably find that your muscle has stretched a little and will allow you to go further next time.

You should follow a familiar and comfortable routine of warm-ups and stretching. After a time, you may

Calf stretch

Calf stretches help to provide the elasticity that reduces the chances of injury and improves performance.

learn a particular routine that stretches all the major muscles and which is most suitable for your particular sport.

STRETCHES

Upper calf

Stand about 1m (3ft) away from a wall and lean forwards to place both palms of the hands on the wall, with your arms at right angles to the wall.

Keep both feet flat on the ground. Lift one heel off the ground by bending a knee while keeping the other leg straight and foot flat on the ground. Bend your elbows until you feel the calf of your supporting leg stretch (keep your heel on the floor). Repeat the process with the other leg.

Lower calf

Lower calf stretch: stand close to the wall and bend one leg. Keep the other foot flat on the floor. To intensify the stretch, lean towards the wall.

Iliotibial stretches

Through strengthening the muscles, iliotibial stretches help to reduce the danger of iliotibial fatigue from running or walking.

Iliotibial band

Stand sideways to the wall with your left hip closest to the wall. Cross your right leg in front of your left leg, keeping both feet flat on the ground.

Move your hip to the left, until you feel a stretch.

Repeat the exercise for the other leg, crossing your left leg in front of your right and moving your hips to the right.

Shins

Kneel with your ankles and feet together. Lower your body slowly until you are sitting on your heels. While keeping your ankles down, keep them together.

Groin

Sit on the ground and pull the soles of your feet together. Place your hands on your feet and rest your elbows on your knees or thighs. Keep

Groin stretch

This stretch is especially important for sports and activities that require stretching and reaching with the legs.

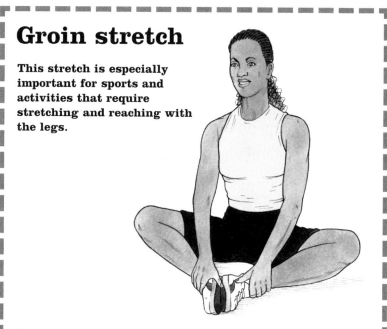

your back straight. Gradually force your knees towards the ground, assisting with a push from your elbows. You should feel a stretch in your groin.

Buttocks

Lie on your back with your left leg straight. Bend your right leg until it comes back towards your hip. Move your right heel towards your left hip. Hold your right ankle with your left hand and your right knee with your right hand. Pull the leg towards your shoulders until you

feel the stretch in your right buttock. Repeat the process for your left buttock.

Hamstring

Lie on your back with one leg straight. Bend the knee of the other leg and bring it back towards the hip. While the knee is bent, grasp the hamstring of the raised leg. Straighten the leg until you feel a stretch in the hamstring. Alternatively, sit on the ground with both legs stretched out in front of you. Bend the left leg and position

Hamstring stretch

This is a vital stretch for a variety of sports, including running, and it also helps reduce the danger of lower back stiffness.

the sole of the left foot alongside the knee of the right leg. Keeping your back straight, bend forwards until you feel the stretch in the hamstring of the right leg. Repeat with the other leg.

Thigh

Lie on your stomach with one leg bent at 90° and the other straight. Place a rope or a towel round the raised ankle and hold with both hands. Push against the towel with the raised leg until you feel the stretch in your thigh. Then repeat with the other leg.

Hip and thigh stretch

Stand straight with your feet about two shoulder widths apart. Turn your feet to the right and face in that direction. Bend your left leg until your right thigh is horizontal. Place your hands on your right knee and lower yourself, bending the right knee and stretching your left leg out behind you until you feel the stretch in the front of the left thigh and hamstrings of the right leg. Repeat the process facing the other way.

Standing quadriceps stretch

Stand upright and bend one leg at the knee. Catch your foot and flex it against your hands until you feel

Quadriceps stretch

This stretch will help you to warm up and improve elasticity in the thigh area before taking exercise.

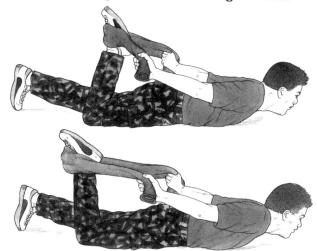

Gluteal stretch

Like the groin stretch, this exercise is important for sports and activities that involve stretching and reaching.

the stretch through the front of your leg.

Kneeling quadriceps stretch
Put your back against a wall and pull one foot and shin up behind you

until you can flatten them against the wall. Lean your body back to maximize the stretch.

Lying quadriceps stretch
Lie on your front, holding a towel or

something similar that you can loop round one foot. Push your foot against the towel until you feel the stretch in the quadriceps.

Cross-leg sitting gluteal stretch
Sit on the ground and cross your legs with your back straight. Push your feet out as far to the side as possible. Bend forwards with arms outstretched.

Biceps and chest stretch
Stand straight with your feet spaced so that they are slightly wider than the width of your shoulders. Hold both arms horizontally and straight with the palms of your hands facing forwards. Rotate your hands so the palms are to the rear. Stretch your arms back until you feel the stretch across your chest and biceps.

Upper back stretch
Stand straight with your feet spaced slightly wider than the width of your shoulders. Bend your knees slightly. Lock your fingers together and push your hands away from your chest until you feel the stretch between the shoulder blades.

Shoulder stretch
Stand straight with your feet spaced slightly wider than the width of your shoulders. Place your right arm horizontally across your chest and use your left forearm to pull the right

Shoulder stretch

There are a variety of shoulder stretches designed to relax this vital part of the upper body.

arm closer to your chest until you feel the stretch in the shoulder. Repeat for the other arm.

Shoulder and triceps stretch
Stand straight with your feet spaced slightly wider than the width of your shoulders. Hold both hands above your head and then slide

them down the middle of your spine until you feel the stretch in your shoulders and triceps.

Side bends
Stand straight with your feet spaced slightly wider than the width of your shoulders. Place your hands on your hips and bend slowly to one side and

Running

back to the upright position. Then bend the other way and repeat.

Adductor stretch

Stand straight and spread your legs out to the equivalent of double your shoulder width. Bend your right leg, using your arms for balance, until you feel the stretch in the left adductor.

RUNNING

Running provides the essential core fitness that forms a base for most other activities and sports. A running programme meshes very well with other sports, including swimming, cycling and skiing, and with other fitness activities such as weights. The advantage of mixing in these

A correct running posture involves a relatively straight back, with opposite arm and leg moving together. This ensures the trunk of the body remains stable while all the energy is channelled into the movement of the legs.

TIP:
BENEFITS OF RUNNING

The benefits of running are many and include:
- Creates a sense of confidence
- Promotes a positive perspective, since in running you are always moving forwards, whether quickly or slowly, as a result of your effort
- Reduces stress – problems often fall into perspective when running, and a feeling of fitness enhances the sense of being able to cope
- Promotes blood and oxygen circulation during and after running, which helps you to think more effectively and make decisions more quickly
- Controls blood pressure and strengthens the cardiovascular system
- Improves the immune system
- Strengthens muscles and bones
- Burns excess fat and maintains optimum weight
- Promotes the human growth hormone
- Raises HDL, or beneficial, cholesterol
- Develops the lungs
- Clears the skin pores and promotes healthy skin

other activities into a running programme is that they add variety, prevent boredom and reduce wear and tear on the legs. Other sports and activities can also complement and improve core strength, which will improve your running posture and performance.

For the purposes of this book, which is about achieving an optimum physical and mental state for emergencies, a running programme to maintain a high level of physical fitness should typically be 30 minutes run between three and five times a week at a reasonable pace. Anyone who chooses to do more than this is probably doing so because he or she is training for races and is therefore an athlete as opposed to a fitness or

TIP:
EFFECTS OF ALCOHOL ON PHYSICAL PERFORMANCE

The ACSM recommends that you should not drink alcohol within 48 hours of taking exercise or undergoing training, if you want to be free from the negative effects of alcohol. If you want to perform to your best, you need to be aware of how your lifestyle will affect your performance. The following tips are based on information provided by BUPA, a British healthcare organization:

- Alcohol increases the likelihood of dehydration.
- Alcohol upsets your natural body temperature monitoring system. This makes it more difficult to cool down after exercise.
- Alcohol lowers your blood sugar level, meaning you have less energy (despite the fact that after a few drinks you might feel like Superman).
- Alcohol adversely affects your speed of reaction, coordination and balance.
- Alcohol is no use as an energy source.
- Alcohol has no useful nutritional value.
- Alcohol impairs vitamin absorption, particularly B group vitamins. Vitamin B (Thiamine), for example, is important for the heart muscle, it stimulates brain activity, maintains the red blood count, improves circulation, reduces fatigue and increases stamina.
- Alcohol undermines your ability to sleep well and will often cause you to wake up in the night.
- Alcohol adversely affects your judgement and physical co-ordination.

Quad lifts

This exercise is designed to strengthen the muscles in your thighs and the quad muscles that support your knee. It is a good exercise for any sport or activity that involves running.

leisure runner. Running schedules also need to take account of the other activities. For example, if you are already engaged in additional exercises, such as regular walking, or practise other sports, you will need to adjust your running programme accordingly. Some experts say it is not a good idea to run on consecutive days, as the body will not have time to recover. The alternative is to run hard on some days and more gently on others.

Choosing a time

The time of day you choose to run will, of course, depend on your commitments. If you have to catch an early train to work, it is unlikely you will have time to fit in a run before.

As far as objective advice goes regarding the optimum time of day to run, there are no hard and fast rules, but common sense dictates that running later in the day places less of a strain on the body due to the fact that your body will be warmed up and your blood sugar level will be at a better level to cope with exertion. In the early morning, your blood sugar level is low and your muscles tend to be colder and stiffer.

If morning runs are the only option, due to other commitments during the day and evening, take care to do some gentle warming-up and eat a nutritious breakfast, including fibre and carbohydrates. A banana or an energy bar will help boost your blood-sugar level.

Run for your life

It has been said that a journey of a thousand miles begins with a single step. For some people, the first part of their training programme for a marathon is a jog to the end of a short street.

Running is the base of both your physical and mental preparation, as it will boost both physical and mental qualities simultaneously. Apart from anything else, running has been shown to have a wide variety of health benefits.

The psychological benefits are numerous as well. You do not pick yourself out of bed and go for a run without a certain amount of character and determination, and these will become second nature as you maintain your running programme.

Running training programme

Running training programmes are almost infinitely variable, depending on your fitness level, age, size, weight, interests, the kind of distances you are interested in, and so on.

As an example, let's consider someone with an average to good level of fitness, who is training for 10km (6 miles) at a moderate level of exertion. A six-week training schedule might look like this:

Week	Date	Mon	Tues	Weds
1	6-12 July	Rest/ cross training	Easy Run - Distance 3.2 km (2 miles)	Rest/ cross training
2	13-19 July	Rest/ cross training	Easy Run - Distance 3.2 km (2 miles)	Rest/ cross training
3	20-26 July	Rest/ cross training	Easy Run - Distance 3.2 km (2 miles)	Rest/ cross training
4	27 July- 2 Aug	Rest/ cross training	Easy Run - Distance 3.2 km (2 miles)	Rest/ cross training
5	3-9 Aug	Rest/ cross training	Easy Run - Distance 3.2 km (2 miles)	Rest/ cross training
6	10-16 Aug	Rest/ cross training	Easy Run - Distance 3.2 km (2 miles)	Rest/ cross training

WALKING

Walking is sometimes overlooked as the most basic form of exercise. Walking of any kind provides some form of cardiovascular exercise, but it needs to be done with a degree of intensity if you are to increase your cardiovascular fitness.

There are various ways of increasing the intensity of walking. You can gradually increase the distances you walk. (You may want to invest in a decent pair of walking shoes or boots to give yourself greater comfort, protection and walking range. See the later section

Thurs	Fri	Sat	Sun
Tempo Run - Distance 8 km (5 miles)	Rest/ cross training	Rest/ cross training	Long Run - Distance 9.7km (6 miles)
Speedwork - Distance 8 km (5 miles)	Rest/ cross training	Rest/ cross training	Long Run - Distance 9.7 km (6 miles)
Tempo Run - Distance 8 km (5 miles)	Rest/ cross training	Rest/ cross training	Long Run - Distance 11.3 km (7 miles)
Easy Run - Distance 4.8 km (3 miles)	Rest/ cross training	Rest/ cross training	Easy Run - Distance 6.4 km (4 miles)
Tempo Run - Distance 9.7 km (6 miles)	Rest/ cross training	Rest/ cross training	Long Run - Distance 11.3 km (7 miles)
Speedwork - Distance 8 km (5 miles)	Rest/ cross training	Rest/ cross training	Long Run - Distance 12.8 km (8 miles)

on equipment and footwear.) You can walk in hilly country, which will provide a greater level of resistance as you walk uphill, thus increasing the physical demands. You can walk with a pack and gradually increase the load in the pack as your fitness improves.

Even if you are involved with other cardiovascular exercises, such as running, cycling or swimming, walking provides a good alternative routine. Walking also has other benefits, as you can normally enjoy the landscape more when you are walking than when you are running.

Wilderness walks

Walking in wild and beautiful places enhances your physical as well as your mental wellbeing.

TIP:
BENEFITS OF WALKING

- Reduces the risk of heart disease and stroke
- Lowers blood pressure
- Reduces cholesterol levels and improves the blood lipid profile
- Reduces body fat
- Enhances mental wellbeing
- Increases bone density, which helps to prevent osteoporosis
- Reduces the risk of cancer of the colon
- Reduces the risk of non-insulin dependent diabetes
- Helps to control body weight
- Increases flexibility and coordination

SWIMMING

Swimming is an excellent all-round cardiovascular exercise. It has an extra benefit due to the fact that the body is supported and protected by the water, which means that it can also be used as a healing therapy for damaged or strained muscles and ligaments. Swimming also complements other sports. It can be used to develop upper-body strength and build-up the lungs as a complement to running, for example.

As with any other sport, swimming requires adequate warm-up and cool-down. Continue the warm-up once you are in the water. Swimming requires more technical skill than running, and it is worth getting the advice of a coach in order to get the most out of your strokes. The two most basic swimming strokes are breaststroke and crawl.

Breaststroke
To perform breaststroke efficiently, try to keep your body as level as possible, with your shoulders in line with your hips. Perhaps the simplest part of breaststroke is the arm movement. It can, however, be more difficult to synchronize the movement of the legs. If you have problems with this aspect of the movement, get into a pool and hold the side or rail with your hands. Then bend your knees and bring your feet up to touch your bottom. Flatten your feet against the water and then push back, as if you were pushing away a flat board with

Breast stroke

Breast stroke is perhaps the most straightforward swimming stroke and one that makes breathing easy.

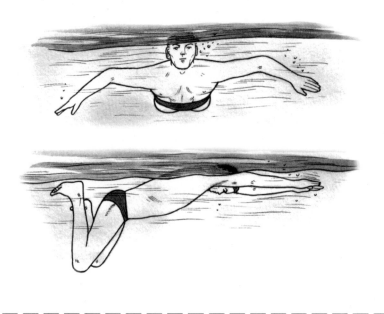

your feet. Your feet should move outwards and then inwards to meet again, with your knees facing each other.

To practise the arm movement, put both arms straight out in front of you, just below the surface of the water. Make sure your hands remain in view at all times. With the backs of your hands against each other, make a wide sweep, pushing the water as you go. Keep your hands slightly cupped. You hands should make a full circle.

As your hands come back towards your chest, you should lift your face out of the water and take a breath of air. As you stretch your arms forward

again, before repeating the circular movement, your face goes back into the water. The arms and legs are coordinated so that when your arms are fully stretched out in front of you to begin the circle, your feet should be against your bottom, ready to kick out. You then kick out and sweep with your arms. You are in a flat position when your arms are stretched out in front of you, but as you pull your arms round in a circle you also exert a lifting movement so that your head and shoulders come out of the water. As you do this, your elbows move from being flat on the surface of the water to being tucked into your chest.

TIP:
BENEFITS OF SWIMMING

- 30 minutes of steady lane swimming burns more than 200 kcal.
- 30 minutes of activity in the water corresponds to 45 minutes of a similar activity on land.
- Swimming is good for body toning.
  Swimming benefits the heart, which has to pump blood to both arms and legs.
- Swimming is good for your lungs because you need to breathe in a deep and rhythmic way.
- Swimming can help to soothe away stress and muscular tension.

Basic Swimming Workout	
Discipline	**Time**
Warm-up: easy 50 metres kick; moderate 50 metres swim; rest 20 seconds. Repeat for full time period.	9 minutes
Refresh skills: easy 25 metres stroke practice; rest for 15 seconds. Repeat for full time period.	9 minutes
Main set: fast 25 metres swim; 25 metres easy swim; fast 25 metres swim; rest 30 seconds. Repeat for full time period.	22 minutes
Cool-down: easy 25 metres swim; rest for 10 seconds. Repeat for full time period.	5 minutes
	Total: 45 minutes

Front crawl

Front crawl is the fastest stroke. The most difficult aspect of the crawl is probably the breathing because, unlike breaststroke, the head is not lifted fully clear of the water.

As with breaststroke, try to keep your body as flat as possible in the water and as close to the surface as possible. Keep your legs slightly bent and move the whole leg when kicking. The kicks may be fast and shallow at the start. Extend one arm at a time straight in front of you. Slice your hand cleanly into the water thumb first. Bend your elbow and swing your hand towards your feet until it reaches your hip. At this point, you lift your arm out of the water and stretch it back once again in front of your head, while the other arm mirrors the underwater motion on the other side of your body.

Apart from synchronizing your limbs, the tricky part of front crawl is to breathe regularly. As your face is naturally in the water, mostly facing the bottom of the swimming pool, you need to turn your head out of the water to get a breath. To do this naturally, so that you get enough oxygen without interrupting your stroke, will require considerable practice. You can try taking a breath every two strokes on your right side. You can experiment with taking a breath every three strokes to see if this works for you.

TRIATHLON

Triathlon is a continuous race covering three disciplines – swimming, cycling and running, in that order. Apart from the skills required for these three disciplines, experts who hope to do well need to master the art of transition from one discipline to another.

The swim/bike/run distances for various kinds of triathlon are:

Super sprint:
400m/10km/2.5km

Sprint distance:
750m/20km/5km

Standard distance:
1500m/40km/10km

Middle distance:
2.5km/80km/20km

Ironman distance:
3.8km/180km/42km

CYCLING

Cycling complements running and other sports because it enables you to exercise major muscles while supporting the body's weight. Take care to use the optimum size of frame for your body and adjust the seat height and handlebars accordingly. Sitting on the saddle, your leg should be almost straight when the pedal is at its lowest point – there should be a slight bend at the knee. To assess the

Cycling

An incorrectly aligned bike seat can seriously impede performance. Correct measurement of saddle height will make for optimum leg power on the bicycle pedals.

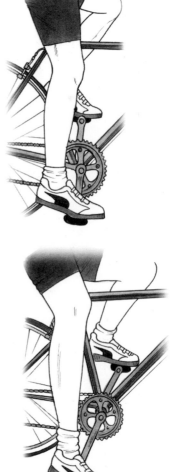

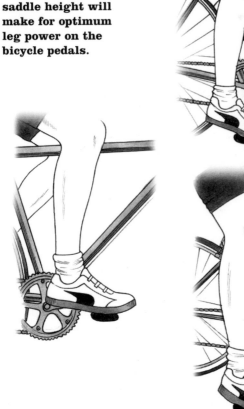

correct position of the handlebars, place your elbow against the front end of the saddle and point your arm towards the handlebars. Place your other hand across your fingertips at 90°. The outside of the little finger on the hand at 90° is approximately the position your handlebars should be. This position may depend, however, on your intended use of the bike. Touring bikes have their handlebars set about level with the saddle, while racing bikes have them set about 5–8cm (2–3in) below the saddle.

If you are training on a bike, particularly in the winter or in the dark, make sure you have lights and high visibility clothing.

ROWING

Rowing is another excellent cardiovascular exercise that provides training for both legs and arms. If you are not near a river, you can still enjoy the benefits of rowing by using a rowing machine. There are obvious differences between rowing in a boat or sculls and a rowing machine, mainly due to the fact that boat oars need to be lifted out of the water, which makes for a different elbow movement. However, rowing is an exercise that depends more on the legs than arms. Surprising though it may seem, at least 70 per cent of the effort when rowing correctly comes from the legs. The arms do the rest. On a rowing machine, begin with arms

Rowing machine

Rowing can be performed either in a boat or on a rowing machine. It provides a good workout for both the legs and the back.

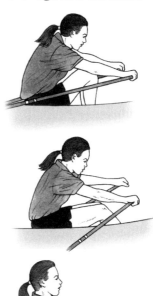

parallel with the ground and the oars or handle pulled in towards your midriff. Your legs should be at full stretch and you should also be leaning back slightly.

Next, move your body forwards, rotating from the hips, with your arms fully extended. Bring the whole of your body forwards on the sliding seat until your legs are against your chest. Your lower legs should be 90 degrees from the floor. Now push back with your legs while leaning back with your upper body to enhance the pull. Keep your arms straight while you push backwards. Once you have pushed back fully, you can bend your arms to finish the pull.

CIRCUIT TRAINING

Circuit training improves strength, stamina and mobility and dovetails well with other activities such as running or swimming. The circuit can involve up to 10 separate exercises that are performed consecutively, with rest periods built in. Obviously the number of repetitions on each exercise and the number of times the circuit is performed will depend on individual levels of fitness.

The circuit is organized so that you exercise different muscle groups, one after the other. So as you exercise one muscle group you give another muscle group a rest. Make sure you warm-up and cool-down before and after circuit training. Typical circuit training exercises are as follows (with the targeted body area indicated in parentheses):

Press-ups (upper body)
Place your hands flat on the ground with your arms and back straight. Lower your body until your chin is near the ground and then push back up again to the original position. Repeat.

Sit-ups (core and trunk)
Lie on the ground or a mat with knees bent, with feet flat on the ground about 8cm (3in) apart. Bend your arms back and place your fingertips near your temples. Raise your body until you are upright. Repeat.

Burpees (full body)
Stand upright. Bend your knees and lower your body to a squat. Support

Press-ups

Press-ups help to strengthen the arms, back and chest.

yourself with your hands on the ground. Extend your legs together as if you were entering a press-up position. Pull your legs back again until your knees are under your chest. Stand up and then repeat the process.

Pull-ups (upper body)
Hang from a bar with your feet clear of the ground. Pull your body up until your chin is level with or over the bar. Lower until your upper arms and forearms are at 90°, then repeat.

Treadmills (full body)
Get into the press-up position. Bring one leg up towards your chest, then return it to the extended position. Do the same thing with the other leg, and so on.

Squat thrusts (lower body)
Get into a crouching position with

Circuit training

Circuit training is designed to exercise muscle groups in the lower and upper body in a co-ordinated way.

This circuit includes: jumping from a squatting position, kneeling leg raises, press ups, raised knee sit-ups, kneeling leg extensions, and standing squats.

Crunches

Crunches exercise and strengthen the abdominal muscles and improve support for the back.

both hands flat on the ground. Shoot both legs back to an extended position and then back to under your chest. Repeat.

Crunches (core and trunk)

- Lie on your back with knees bent and both feet flat on the ground. Put your hands behind your head. Lift your shoulders slowly off the floor, hold for about four seconds, then lower yourself back to the floor again.
- Lie on your back with knees bent, both feet on the ground and hands behind your head. Move one hand towards the foot on the same side, keeping the other hand behind your head. Repeat with the other hand.
- Lie on your back with knees bent, both feet flat on the floor and your hands behind your head. Bring one knee up towards your chest and try to touch it with the elbow on the other side of your body. Balance yourself with the other leg, stretching it out straight. Repeat on the opposite side of the body.
- Lie on your back, and then lift your legs until they are 90° from the ground. Rest the small of your back on the ground. Tighten and relax your stomach muscles.

Pull-ups

Pull ups are a good way of strengthening the dorsal muscles in the back as well as the muscles of the arms.

WEIGHT TRAINING

Never start or finish weight training without a proper warm-up and cool-down. Weight training can place a considerable pressure on the heart, so build up your training slowly and seek professional advice when using heavy weights.

Weight training is sometimes confused with body building. Weight training is actually about strengthening groups of muscles for optimum performance in various sports, whereas body building has more to do with visible physique. Experiments have shown that if you take a group of athletes training for a particular sport, such as long-distance running, and you divide them between those who use running plus weight training, the group using weight training performed better overall. This superiority is because the performance of one discipline or sport will not necessarily in itself develop the muscles in an optimum way.

Weight training builds muscle and increases power. Upper-body weight training is useful for runners because a) running exercises the legs and not the upper body, and b) a well-toned upper body will provide the optimum posture for effective running. Well-developed stomach muscles support the back and help to keep it erect.

Bench presses

Working with heavy weights builds up muscle power but should be performed only under professional supervision and using the correct equipment.

TIP:
STRENGTH TRAINING
– DUMBELL EXERCISES

Exercise 1

Hold dumbbells by your side, with the top of your hands facing upwards. Raise one dumbbell with your arm straight until your arm is horizontal. Lower the dumbbell and then raise the other one. Repeat the set.

Exercise 2

Bend forwards, keeping your back straight. Raise both dumbbells until both arms are horizontal, then lower them again. Repeat.

Exercise 3

Stand straight with your feet slightly apart. Hold both dumbbells at shoulder height and take turns to raise each one above your head.

Exercise 4

Stand straight with both dumbbells by your side with arms straight. With the back of your hand facing the ground, raise each dumbbell in turn to chest height.

Exercise 5

Stand straight with the dumbbells by your side. Raise both arms simultaneously, with the back of your hand upwards until your arms are horizontal. Lower the dumbbells back to your side and repeat.

Lateral curls

This exercise will work your shoulder muscles. Raise your arms until they are horzontal, then lower again.

Tricep lifts

The triceps is on the back of the upper arm. With one knee resting on a stool, lean forwards and raise the weight by straightening your arm.

Bicep curls

Rest your elbow on your knee. Lift the weight in towards the body.

As with much of the advice in this book, practice makes perfect. If you are faced with a first aid emergency, it will be a huge advantage if you have practised the relevant techniques beforehand so that you do not waste valuable time. In most countries, first aid and accident prevention courses are run by many local and national organizations. Those who are involved with the Scout Association or the Guide Association, or the armed forces, for example, are likely to be able to access first aid training through these groups.

There are certain basic routines to follow when faced with an accident or emergency involving a wounded person. They should become second nature if you practise them enough. The key points (which are explained in further detail below) are:

- Is it safe to help?
- Examine the patient.
- ABC (Airway, Breathing, Circulation) priorities.
- If necessary, administer immediate resuscitation.
- Place the patient in the recovery position (if appropriate).
- Stabilize the condition and get help.

. . . .

Left: Learning a variety of key first aid techniques is crucial preparation for crisis survival.

7

Knowing how to deal with injuries in a crisis situation will save lives.

Preparation

First Aid

IS IT SAFE?

You need to check whether it is safe to approach an injured person. For example, he or she may be on a road; there may be flammable liquids about, such as petrol; there may be live electric wires or cables; the casualty may be near a rockfall that is still hazardous. If it is safe to approach but the casualty is in a potentially dangerous place, you may need to move him. However, you will need to check whether he has suffered a spinal injury, in which case he should not be moved unless absolutely necessary.

ABC (Airway, Breathing, Circulation)

Easy to remember, the 'ABC' letters will let you make a rapid assessment of the patient's condition and provide essential treatment as soon as possible. If the patient can speak and respond to a simple question like 'How are you?', this obviously makes the process more straightforward. If he cannot speak, is unconscious or in visible distress, go through the following routine:

Airway
Check for signs of airway blockage,

Checking breathing

Lift the casualty's chin to open the airway and place your ear near the mouth and nose to check for breathing.

clear the mouth of obstructions such as blood, vomit or anything else. Check that the tongue is not blocking the throat. Tilt the head gently back and lift the chin – this action opens the airway.

Breathing

Look for obvious signs of breathing, such as the chest rising and falling. If nothing is visible, put your ear near to the nose and mouth of the patient to detect the sound of breath. Hold your hand near to the nose and mouth to check whether you can feel breath. If there is no sign of breathing, you must take immediate action, as below (artificial respiration).

Circulation

Check for a pulse at the neck or on the underside of the wrist. If there is

Checking a pulse

You can check a pulse either on the underside of the wrist or by holding two fingers against the carotid artery in the neck.

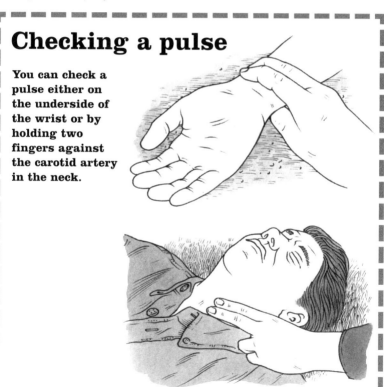

no pulse, you should administer Cardiopulmonary Resuscitation (CPR). Check the colour of the patient's skin.

ARTIFICIAL RESPIRATION

If the patient is not breathing, artificial respiration must be given urgently. After clearing the airway of any blockages and ensuring the patient is on a firm surface, tilt the patient's head gently back and place the heel of your hand on his forehead. Using the hand on the forehead, hold the patient's nose closed with thumb and forefinger. Open the mouth with your other hand. Take a deep breath, place your mouth tightly over the patient's mouth and exhale. When the patient's chest is fully expanded, stop blowing. Lift your hand from the victim and wait

Giving CPR

CPR should be performed only if there is no pulse. Place the heel of the hand on the lower part of the breastbone and the other hand on top of that. Press the breastbone 80 times per minute. Pause every 15 presses to give the casualty two breaths. Check the pulse and then continue if necessary.

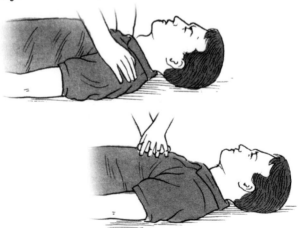

for the chest to fall. Then give the patient further breaths of air at a rate of 12 breaths per minute. When the patient begins to breathe on his own, stop the resuscitation process.

CARDIO-PULMONARY RESUSCITATION (CPR)

Use this method only if there is no pulse. If there is a trace of a pulse, CPR should not be used. You should perform CPR only if you have had training. If there is no pulse and you have performed artificial respiration, place the heel of one hand on the lower part of the breastbone and the other hand on top of that. Taking care not to damage the ribs, press the breastbone down at a cyclical rate of 80 times per minute, pausing every 15 presses to give the patient two breaths (see page 100 for artificial

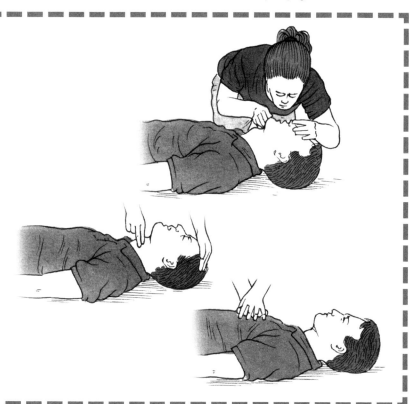

TIP: CPR ON INFANTS

CPR *for a baby*: place two fingers on the breastbone.
Press down sharply to a depth of 2cm (0.8in). Press five
times in three seconds. Perform one breath of artificial
respiration, with your mouth enclosing both the baby's
mouth and nose. Perform this routine (CPR + AR) for a
whole minute. Continue until help arrives or the baby
starts breathing.

CPR *for a young child*: Place your middle finger on the
tip of the breastbone and your index finger on the bone
above it. Slide the heel of your other hand down the
breastbone to meet your fingers. Use the heel of your
hand on its own to push down to a depth of 3cm (1.2in).
Repeat five times in three seconds. Give one full breath of
artificial respiration (holding the nose closed as for an
adult). Repeat this routine for one minute. Continue if
there is no improvement. If pulse and breathing return,
place child in the recovery position (see page 104).

respiration). If you have someone to
help you, they can perform the
artificial respiration while you pause
from the CPR. One breath should be
given for every five compressions.
You should give 60 compressions per
minute with a pause of one to one-
and-a-half seconds after every five
compressions.

EXAMINATION TECHNIQUE

When performing an examination of
an injured person, follow the
sequence: Look, Feel, Listen. If you
are checking a limb joint, the
sequence is Look, Feel, Move.

When examining a patient, take into
account his weight, fitness, skin tone
and psychological state. Lay the
patient down for the examination, and
reassure them with a soothing voice.

Starting from the right of the body,
examine the following:
Hands – check nails and palms for
anaemia.
Pulse – check the rate, rhythm and
volume.
Blood pressure – hypotension is
low; hypertension is high.

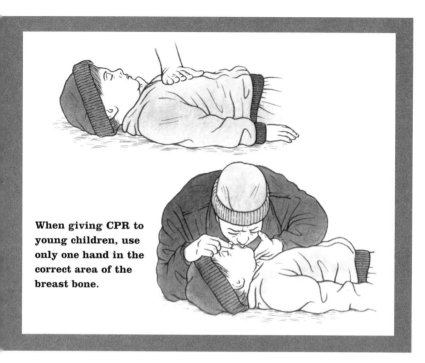

When giving CPR to young children, use only one hand in the correct area of the breast bone.

Head – eyes, ears, lips and mouth.
Neck – check whether it is broken or bruised.
Chest – lungs and heart.
Abdomen – liver, spleen and kidneys.
Limbs – look, feel, move.

SHOCK

Circulatory shock (as opposed to psychological shock) results from a lowering of blood pressure, which is in turn the result of a reduced blood volume circulating to vital body organs, such as the brain, heart, liver and kidneys. It is caused primarily by injures that are bleeding, but there are other causes. Burn wounds will result in loss of plasma. Vomiting or diarrhoea will result in loss of body water. Pain and anxiety will make things worse.

Symptoms of shock
- Pale, cold and sweaty skin with a grey tinge.
- Pulse that is rapid and also weakening.
- Shallow, fast breathing.
- Dilated eye pupils.

TIP:
RECOVERY POSITION

Beware moving a patient who may have a spine injury. If
he does have a spinal injury, the back and spine should be
immobilized before moving him. Otherwise, follow these
steps to place the patient in the recovery position:

- Turn his head towards you, tilting it back slightly to
  open the airway.
- Place the arm nearest to you by the side of the patient
  and slide it under their buttock.
- Lay the other arm across the patient's chest.
- Place the leg that is furthest away across the one that
  is nearest at the ankle.
- Roll the patient gently towards you by grasping
  clothing around the hip with one hand. Support the
  head with the other hand.
- Rest the victim against your knees.
- Bend the top-side leg so that the body does not roll
  too much.
- Keep the head tilted back to maintain an open airway.

The recovery position puts the casualty on his front
(although the bent leg keeps the chest off the floor) to
ensure drainage of fluids away from the lungs and ease
of breathing.

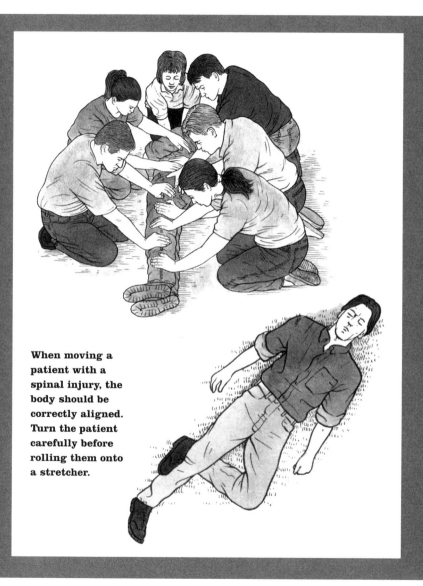

When moving a patient with a spinal injury, the body should be correctly aligned. Turn the patient carefully before rolling them onto a stretcher.

- The patient may yawn and sigh, may complain of being thirsty and may lose consciousness.

Treatment for shock

Lay the victim down and elevate her legs (supporting them on a cushion or other object) – keep her head low. Loosen any clothing around the neck, chest and waist, and use a blanket or something similar to provide moderate warmth (do not provide direct heat). Control any bleeding and provide pain relief as necessary, but do not give food or drink. If you are qualified to do so, and have the means, replace fluid intravenously. Call for medical assistance and evacuate by stretcher.

CHOKING

Choking is caused by a blockage of the airway, usually by food. The signs are that a person suddenly clutches at his throat, and may be unable to speak, breathe or cough. He may emit a wheezing sound, his skin and lips of the face may even go blue,

Treating shock

If shock is caused by loss of blood, lifting the legs helps to concentrate the flow of blood around the torso.

Treating choking

If the casualty is conscious, try five firm slaps on the back. If they are unconscious, make abdominal thrusts below the rib cage and above the navel.

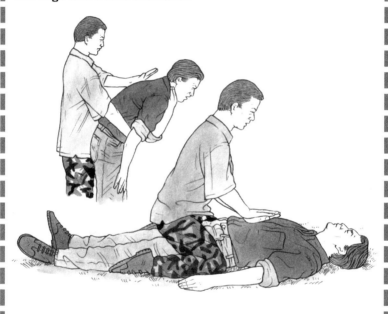

and, if he is unconscious, his chest will not be visibly rising or falling.

Treating a conscious victim for choking

- Lower patient's head to below chest level.
- Give five firm slaps to the back to dislodge the obstruction.

If no improvement:

- Stand behind patient and place one fist just under the breastbone or sternum.
- Hold the fist cupped in the other hand and make a sharp, hard thrusting movement inwards and upwards. This technique is known as the Heimlich Manoeuvre and

works by forcing air up the windpipe and, hopefully, popping the obstruction from the throat.

If you are the person choking and you are on your own:

- Use your own hands to administer abdominal thrusts.
- Lean over the back of a chair or, if outside, over a tree stump, placing the edge of the object against your diaphragm. Lower your body weight quickly to force air upwards to clear the obstruction.

Treating an unconscious victim for choking

- Place the heel of your hand against the middle of his abdomen, just above the navel.
- Place the other hand on top and press with a quick upward thrust.
- If the blockage remains, try using your finger to clear the throat or pull it out with foreceps or tweezers. A torch may be useful to see the obstruction.
- If there is no breathing, give artificial respiration.

Treating a baby for choking

- Lay the baby face down along your forearm with his or her head low.
- Give five sharp slaps between the shoulders.

If the obstruction remains:

- Place the baby face up along your other arm.
- Place two fingers on the lower part of the breastbone.
- Give five sharp downward thrusts.
- Look in the mouth, holding the tongue down with one finger.
- Remove the obstruction if visible.
- Carry on with the sequences until the blockage is cleared.

NEAR DROWNING

Symptoms

- Pale and cool skin
- No breathing
- Blue lips (cyanosis)
- Weak or absent pulse
- Unconsciousness

Treatment

Step 1: Check the patient via the ABC method: Airway, Breathing, Circulation.
Step 2: If the patient has no pulse, or is not breathing, deliver CPR. If providing artificial respiration, you may need to breathe more heavily to overcome the effects of water in the lungs.
Step 3: Once the heartbeat and breathing are restored, keep the casualty's head lower than the rest of the body to let water drain from the lungs. If the patient is coughing or spluttering, keep her on her side. If she is unconscious, use the recovery position (see page 104).
Step 4: Call for medical assistance.

Shock and hypothermia can often accompany near drownings. For treatment for both injuries, see page 109 opposite.

COLD INJURIES

Hypothermia

Hypothermia occurs when the body temperature falls below 37°C (99°F). Causes are typically extreme cold, typically combined with wind chill and wet clothing, or immersion in cold water or snow.

Symptoms

- Drowsiness
- Lowered breathing and heart rate
- Unconsciousness

Treatment

- Your priority is urgent warming of the whole body, evenly and gently.
- Replace any wet clothing with clean, dry clothing.
- Place the victim in a sleeping bag in a warm area. If necessary, have another person in the same sleeping bag to improve warmth.
- If the means are available, immerse the person in a warm bath.
- Provide artificial respiration if breathing stops.
- Seek professional medical help.

Treating hypothermia

When treating hypothermia, keep the patient warm and dry with blankets or a sleeping bag.

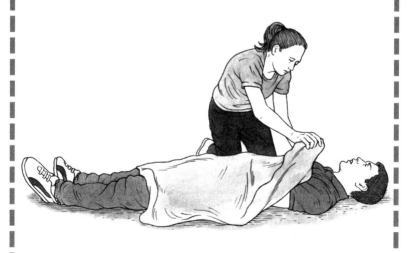

TIP:
HOW TO AVOID FROSTBITE

Frostbite is caused by tissue damage after extreme cold. To avoid frostbite:
- Keep as much of the body covered as possible. Frostbite often affects the extremities (such as fingers and toes) and any exposed areas of the body (such as ears and nose).

To minimize the risk of frostbite:
- Wear insulated boots and at least two pairs of socks.
- Wear thermal gloves on your hands (you can wear inner gloves and outer mittens).
- Wear a lined cap with flaps for ears and / or a balaclava to protect ears and nose.

Frostbite

Frostbite describes what occurs when skin tissue is damaged by exposure to severe cold, the fluid within the exposed skin literally beginning to freeze.

Symptoms
- Pins and needles in the affected area, followed by numbness.
- Skin changes from being white, cold and hard to red and swollen.

Treatment
- Place patient in a warm area and remove clothing from the affected area.
- Put clean, warm clothing on the affected part.
- Keep the affected part warm. If frostbite affects the hand, you can place it under an armpit.
- Seek professional medical help.

Chilblains

Chilblains are caused by lengthy exposure of the skin to low temperatures, causing constriction of the small blood vessels below the surface of the skin. Less severe than frostbite, chillblains are nonetheless an uncomfortable condition.

Symptoms
- Itchy, purple-red swelling on toe or finger.

- Sensation of pins and needles, to numbness.

Treatment
- Warm the affected part (e.g. put cold hands in warm gloves).
- Keep warming until the condition subsides.

TRENCH OR IMMERSION FOOT

This condition is caused by exposure of the feet to wet and damp conditions over a prolonged period.

Symptoms
- Feet turn pale and then red.
- Feet are swollen and painful.

Treatment
If the feet are pale, warm them gently, but if feet are red and swollen, cool them gradually. Do not massage the feet or apply direct heat or cold, and change socks daily to make sure they are clean and dry. If there are no drying facilities, wrap a wet pair of socks round your waist and dry them with body heat.

HEAT INJURIES

There are a number of different types of environmental heat injuries, mostly associated by too much exposure to sun or over-exertion in warm conditions.

Heat cramps

Heat cramps are caused by excessive loss of body salts through sweating, vomiting or diarrhoea.

Symptoms
- Cramps in the arms, legs or abdomen.
- Heavy sweating and thirst.

Treatment
- Move the patient to a cool, shady area.
- Provide drinking water.
- Loosen clothing.
- Seek medical assistance if no improvement.

Heat Exhaustion

Heat exhaustion is caused by an imbalance between sweating and water intake.

Symptoms
- Heavy sweating.
- Pale and clammy skin.
- Headache, dizziness and confusion.

Treatment
- Move the patient to a cool, shady area.
- Provide drinking water.
- Loosen clothing.
- The patient should get plenty of rest.
- Seek medical assistance if no improvement.

Heatstroke

Heatstroke is a life-threatening condition caused by a failure of

Treating heatstroke

The casualty should be taken out of the sun and given cool water to drink. Raising the legs can help blood circulation and reduce dizziness.

body-cooling mechanisms after long exposure to heat and sun.

Symptoms
- Skin becomes red and dry.
- Rapid, weak pulse.
- Headache.
- Dizziness.
- Nausea.

Treatment
- Move the patient to a cool, shaded area.
- Raise and support the legs.
- Provide drinking water if conscious.

- Use water (if enough is available) to cool the victim. Soak the clothing directly and fan to facilitate evaporation.
- Massage the extremities to improve blood flow.
- Monitor patient and provide emergency help if necessary.
- Seek urgent medical assistance.

BURNS
The severity of any burn is classified by a system of degrees, denoting the depth to which the skin is damaged by the burn.

Treating burns

To avoid continued tissue damage, apply cool water to a burn as soon as possible. Keep applying water for at least 10 minutes.

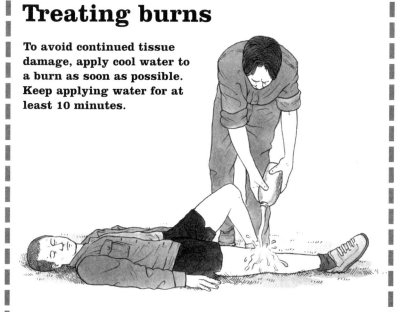

Type of Burn	Damage	Treatment
First Degree	Only top layer of skin affected, e.g. from sunburn. Skin turns red and then peels.	Rehydrating creams. Treatment for restlessness, headache or fever. Cool water at regular intervals.
Second Degree	Deeper damage to the skin, causing blisters and shock.	Use anti-bacterial dressing or leave wound undressed, but keep clean. Treat for shock.
Third Degree	Damage to all layers of skin. Shock.	Requires specialist treatment. Treat for shock until professional help arrives.

Treatment
- Do not remove any clothing that may be sticking to a burn, as this could pull skin away.
- Cool the wound with cool water as soon as possible.
- Attempt to remove clothing only when wound is thoroughly cooled.
- If material remains stuck to the skin, cut clothing away around it.
- Once cooled, cover the burn with clean material (not fluffy). Alternatively, use kitchen film.
- Do not apply ointments, butter or fat to the wound.
- Provide adequate fluid for the patient.

BLEEDING INJURIES

Bleeding can be arterial, venous or capillary, in order of seriousness from worst to least severe. Major blood loss leads to shock (see page 103–6).

Arterial
Blood in the arteries is under high

TIP:
TYPES OF SHOCK

- Circulatory or physiological shock results from a severe reduction of blood volume in the body.

- Psychological shock is the mental stress caused by a traumatic experience. It is sometimes known as post-traumatic stress disorder.

Causes of circulatory shock include:
- loss of blood due to a severe injury or illness
- the widening or obstruction of blood vessels
- burns
- vomiting
- diarrhoea
It can also be caused by a heart attack.

Causes of psychological shock include:
- tragic events that bring on emotional trauma
- natural disasters
- violent incidents
Symptoms may include anxiety, depression and irritability.

pressure and therefore if an artery is ruptured the victim is in danger of a fatal loss of blood and could die within minutes. Arterial blood can be recognized by its bright red colour and by the spurting effect, which is in time with the pumping of the heart.

Venous
Venous blood is more easily controlled than arterial blood, and is a darker shade of red.

Capillary
These blood vessels are opened in minor cuts and grazes, and the bleeding is typically non-serious.

Treatment
Press firmly on the wound to stop the

Applying a pad and bandage

Place a pad with a bandage directly over the wound and tie it securely. If blood seeps through the first bandage, apply another and bandage again.

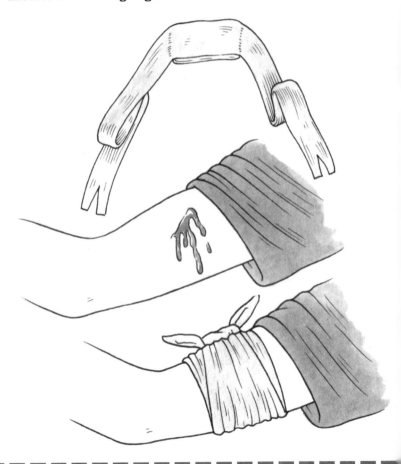

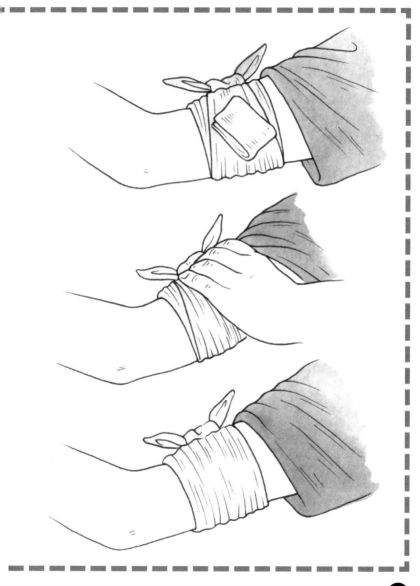

bleeding. Apply the pressure using a dressing, clean pad or handkerchief, or if one of these isn't available put the palm of your hand directly over the wound.

Lay the patient down, with his head low (place something soft under the head if possible) and keep the injured part raised above the heart to reduce the blood pressure at the injury site. Keep pressing on the wound for up to 10 minutes until the bleeding stops.

Cover the wound with a sterile dressing that is larger than the wound. Bandage the dressing in place, keeping the injured part raised. The bandage should be firm but not so tight as to cut off the blood supply.

When the bleeding is under control, support the injury (e.g. with a sling – see below, page 299). Get the casualty to professional medical help.

Applying a tourniquet

Apply a tourniquet in an emergency only, and if there is immediate risk of death by blood loss. Remove the tourniquet as soon as it is safe to do so.

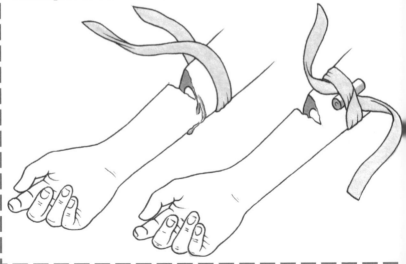

Cuts and grazes

If the cut is slight, rinse the wound in clean water to remove any grit or dirt. Dab it gently with sterile gauze to dry it. Apply a dressing or plaster.

Open wounds

In a survival situation, it is important to try to keep any wound clean. Cover the wound with a clean dressing, which should be changed daily to check for infection. If the wound becomes infected, place a warm, moist compress on it and hold it there for 30 minutes. Allow the wound to drain. Then dress and bandage the wound again. In extreme situations, if maggots get into the wound, leave them for as long as they feed on dead tissue, as this will clean the wound. When the surrounding tissue becomes painful and red, this is a sign that the maggots have begun to feed on live tissue. At this point, flush them out with sterile water or urine.

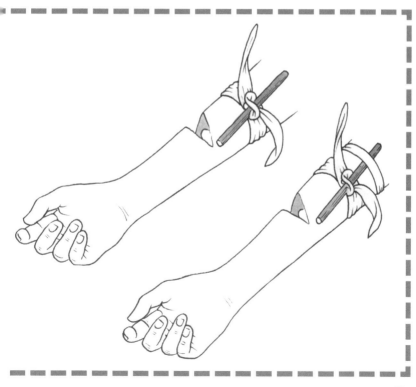

TIP:
APPLYING DRESSINGS

Follow these guidelines to make the most of a dressing:
- Ensure the dressing pad extends beyond the edges of the wound.
- Place the dressing directly on the wound – do not slide it around.
- If blood seeps through the dressing, do not replace it but put another dressing over the top.
- If there is only one sterile dressing, use this one directly on the wound and use others to back it up.

Place the dressing firmly on the wound and bandage carefully. Use a sterile dressing directly on the wound.

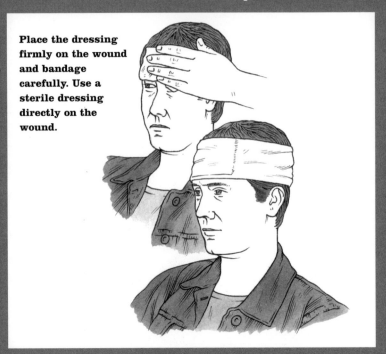

Applying a dressing to an injured limb

- Wind the short end of the bandage once round the limb and the dressing to secure the pad. Leave the end hanging.
- Wind the other end of the bandage round the limb to cover

Support bandage

Roll the bandage carefully both above and below the affected area in order to provide adequate support.

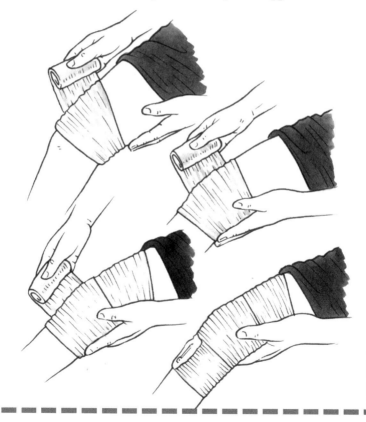

the whole pad, leaving the tail hanging free.

- To secure the bandage, tie the ends in a reef knot over the pad to exert firm pressure over the top of the wound.
- Check the circulation beyond the bandage (press the fingernails or toenails, and ensure that they return to pink when you release the pressure). Loosen the bandage if necessary.
- If nothing else is available and the wound is gaping, close it with adhesive tape, making sure it is sterile and clean first.

Sutures

- If you have experience and clean materials, you can suture the wound.

- Pass the needle into one edge of the skin and out of the other edge.
- Knot each stitch on one side.
- Take in equal amounts of skin on both sides to align the edges of the wound.
- Tie the sutures with a square knot. Loop over the needle holder, then grasp the end through the loop and pull tight. Loop round the needle holder in the other direction, grasp the end through the loop and pull tight again.
- Leave the sutures in place for about 10 days. When you take them out, snip the stitches, grasp the knot with forceps and tweezers and pull the stitch out with a firm pull.

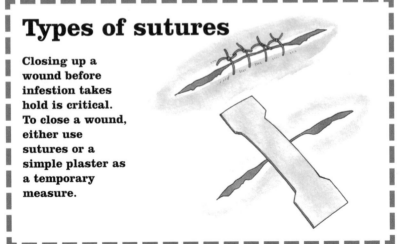

Types of sutures

Closing up a wound before infestion takes hold is critical. To close a wound, either use sutures or a simple plaster as a temporary measure.

Stitching a wound

To stitch a wound, press
the needle into one skin
edge, through the full
depth of the wound and
then out through the other
skin edge. Knot the stitch
on one side of the wound.

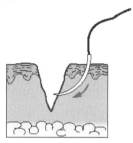

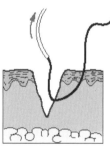

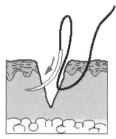

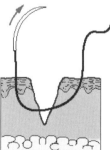

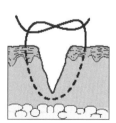

FRACTURES

Symptoms

A fracture is a break in a bone, which is usually caused by a fall or heavy impact. In a closed, or simple, fracture, the broken bone end remains beneath the skin. In an open, or compound, fracture, both ends of bone protrude through the skin. Fractures are recognizable either by a heavily bruised swelling or projecting bone ends. Both types of fracture are very painful.

Treatment

- Do not try to force the bones back together – seek medical assistance.
- Treat open wounds with a clean dressing.
- Splint the fractured area in exactly the way you find it to prevent any further movement.
- If the arm is fractured, splint it and then create a sling if the arm can be held across the chest.
- If you suspect a spinal injury, do not move the patient at all.

Types of fractures

L to R top: Simple fracture; greenstick fracture; comminuted fracture. L to R bottom: Closed fracture; open fracture.

Splints

These can be made out of sticks, tree branches, boards or anything stiff, including a rolled newspaper. The splint must be long enough to immobilize the limb above and below the fracture. First, place a pad between the splint and any boney part of the body. Tie the splint against the limb at four points – two above and two below the fracture. (Tie non-slip knots with the bow on the outside.) If a leg is broken, you can use the other good leg as a support, placing padding between the legs.

Skull fractures

These fractures are potentially very serious and require urgent medical attention.

Symptoms

- Wound or bruise on the head.
- A soft area on the scalp.
- Semi-consciousness or slow responses.
- Clear fluid seeping from nose or ear.
- Blood showing in the white of the eye.
- Distortion of head or face.

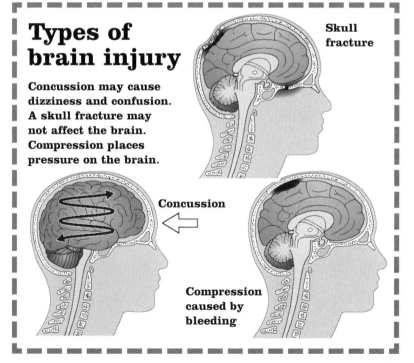

Types of brain injury

Concussion may cause dizziness and confusion. A skull fracture may not affect the brain. Compression places pressure on the brain.

Skull fracture

Concussion

Compression caused by bleeding

Treatment

Place the patient in the recovery position, and get urgent medical assistance. Check for symptoms of circulatory shock and treat accordingly.

Neck fracture
Treatment

Immobilize the neck with a cervical collar or place a rolled towel under the neck to support it, and two heavy objects on either side of the head to keep it stable (e.g. a pair of boots). Do not move the casualty unless absolutely necessary, and keep the head completely still if you do. Get professional medical help as quickly as possible.

Arm fractures
Shoulder blade or collarbone

Use a sling to take the weight off the arm. Immobilize the arm with a bandage round the arm in the sling and back round the body.

Upper arm

Put a pad in the armpit. Place a splint from shoulder to elbow on the outside of the arm. Put a sling round the wrist and neck to support the arm.

Elbow

Support the elbow in a sling if bent. Bind the arm to the body by passing a bandage round the back. If the arm is not bent, support the arm with

Stabilizing the neck

With a neck fracture, it is important to support and immobilize the neck as shown. Try to avoid moving the casualty.

Basic sling

A basic sling is simply looped round the wrist and over the back of the neck.

splints and padding and bind it to the body.

Forearm, hand or fingers

Immobilize the forearm and hand with a splint extending from the elbow to the end of the fingers. Use padding in the splint. Elevate the arm in a sling to prevent swelling.

Leg fracture

Hip or upper leg

Place splints on the inside of the leg, with padding between the splint and injured limb. Now place a longer splint from the ankle to the armpit on the outside of the leg. If there are no splints, use the other leg as a splint with a blanket between.

Knee fracture

Try to make the leg straight if possible, but do not force it. Place a splint below the leg and provide support padding under the knee if it is slightly bent. If the leg is more bent and cannot be straightened,

Bandaging closed fracture

Use the other leg to support the damaged leg. Bandage above and below the fracture area as shown.

Pelvis fracture

Strap the two legs together with padding in between and bandage the feet, ankles, knees and pelvis.

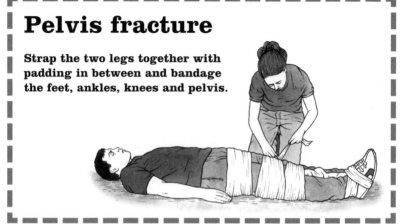

strap the egs together with padding below and above the knee.

Lower leg
Place splints on both sides of the leg, extending from the foot to above the knee. If no splints are available, use the other leg as a splint with padding in between.

Ankle or foot
Raise the injured leg and support it.

Making a stretcher

An emergency stretcher can be constructed by binding the casualty to two strong lengths of wood with padding as shown.

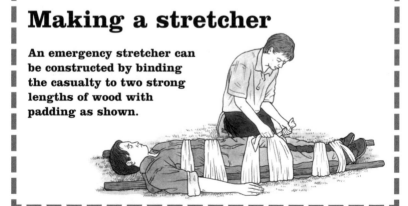

TIP: TREATING A PELVIS FRACTURE

Place a pad between the thighs and tie at the knees and ankles. If the legs are bent, place padding beneath the knees. If possible, the patient can be strapped to a board, or door, with straps at the ankles, waist and top part of the chest, under the arms. If there is no board available, strap the two legs together, with padding between, bandaging at the feet, ankles, knees and pelvis.

Note that a boot will provide some support for the ankle or foot, so leave it on if possible. Try not walk on the injured part.

SLINGS AND BANDAGES

Slings are an ideal way to support and protect an injured limb or joint while you are transporting the casualty to professional help.

Arm sling

Place an open triangular bandage between the body and the arm with one point towards the elbow. Take the upper point over the shoulder on the uninjured side and round the neck. Bring the lower point under, then up, over the arm and tie it to the upper point with a reef knot. Fold any excess bandage over the elbow and

Supporting sling

A sling is an effective means of supporting an injured arm and can be made from any triangular piece of material.

secure it with a safety pin. The wrist should be slightly higher than the elbow.

St John Sling

The elbow should be beside the body and the hand extended towards the uninjured shoulder. Place an open triangular bandage over the forearm and hand with the point towards the elbow. Extend the upper point of the bandage over the uninjured shoulder. Tuck the lower part of the bandage under the injured arm. Bring the lower part of the bandage under the elbow and round the back. Take the lower point of the bandage up to meet the upper point at the shoulder, and tie the ends with a reef knot. Fold the excess material up so that it is snug against the limb and use a safety pin to secure it. Ensure the sling is tucked under the arm and that it gives firm support.

Collar and cuff

Allow the elbow to hang at the side and extend the hand towards the shoulder on the uninjured side. Tie a clove hitch with two loops, one towards you and one away from you. Put the loops together by sliding your hands under the loops and closing with a clapping motion. Now tie a clove hitch directly on the wrist – slide the clove hitch over the hand and gently but firmly pull it to secure the wrist. Extend the points of the bandage to either side of the neck and tie firmly with a reef knot.

Leg bandage

Place the centre of a triangular bandage over the dressing that covers the wound. Take the lower end round and up the leg in a spiral motion and the upper end round and down the leg in a spiral motion, overlapping slightly on each turn. Bring both ends together and tie with a non-slip knot.

Bandaging a foot

A foot can be bandaged with a standard bandage as shown if a triangular bandage is not available.

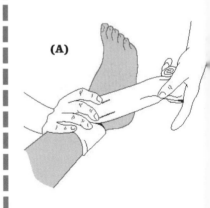

(A)

Foot bandage

Place the injured foot in the middle of a triangular bandage with the heel well forward of the base. Separate the toes with absorbent material to prevent chafing and irritation. Place the forward point of the bandage over the top of the foot and tuck any excess material into the pleats on each side of the foot. Cross the ends on top of the foot, take them round the ankle and tie them at the front of the ankle.

Hand bandage

Place the hand on the bandage with the wrist at the base. Separate fingers with soft material to stop them chafing. Bring the apex of the bandage over the fingers, then bring the ends round to tie at the wrist.

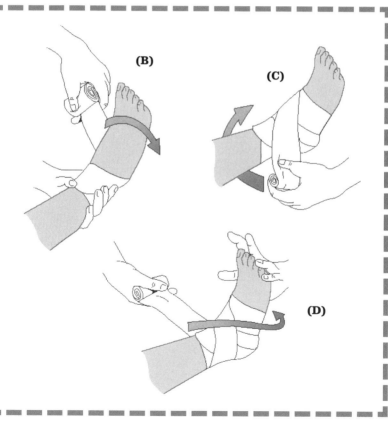

(B)

(C)

(D)

POISONING, BITES AND STINGS

Insect bites or stings

If it is a sting, remove the stinger by scraping the flesh with a knife or similar object. If there is a sack attached to the stinger (as with a bee sting), do not squeeze it (this will inject more poison into the wound). Wash the area with soap and water, and apply an ice pack to reduce spread of poison. If there is a serious reaction to the bite or sting, treat as for snake bite (see box below).

Stings from spiny fish, urchins, stingrays and cone shells

Soak the wound in hot water for

TIP: TREATING A SNAKE BITE

Symptoms – The symptoms vary according to the type of snake. Usual symptoms include: tissue swelling in the area of the bite, which gradually spreads; blood in the urine; severe headaches and thirst; irregular heartbeat; weakness and exhaustion; dizziness; blurred vision; confusion; lack of muscular coordination; twitching; difficulty breathing; tingling; excessive perspiration; numbness in the lips and soles of the feet; nausea; vomiting and diarrhoea; unconsciousness; low blood pressure; and high pulse rate.

Treatment – If the bite is on the arm or leg, place a constricting band above and below the bite. If there is only one band available, place it between the bite and the heart. The bands should be tight enough to prevent the flow of blood near the skin of the affected area, but not so tight as to prevent circulation altogether. Pour clean water over the bite so the water runs away from the body, carrying off the venom. Place an ice pack over the area of the bite and treat the casualty for shock as necessary. Seek medical assistance urgently.

Do not try to suck out the venom, or use ointments on the bite, or give the patient food, coffee or tea, drugs or tobacco.

between 30 minutes and 1 hour in order to de-activate the toxin.

Animal bites

Clean the wound thoroughly by flushing it out with clean water. Cover the wound with a sterile dressing. If an arm or leg is injured, immobilize it. Get medical help urgently and provide detailed information of the type of animal – in some countries, animals are carriers of rabies.

Ingestion of poisonous berries or tablets

Induce vomiting by placing two fingers down the back of the throat.

Pour clean water over the bite to wash poison away.

TREATMENT FOR INTESTINAL WORMS

Prevention – maintain high standards of cleanliness; do not eat uncooked meat or vegetables; wash food carefully.

Treatment – if no worm medicine is available, try:

- *Salt water:* dissolve four tablespoons of salt in 1 litre (2 US / 1¾ UK pints) of water. Drink this only once.
- *Tobacco:* eat the tobacco from one and a half cigarettes. Do not repeat the treatment for at least 24 hours.
- *Kerosene:* take a dose of two tablespoons. Do not inhale the fumes. Do not repeat the treatment for at least 24 hours.
- *Hot peppers:* as a regular part of your diet, these will help to keep parasites at bay.

Ten deadliest natural disasters by death toll

Rank	Event	Location
1.	China floods	China
2.	Yellow River flood	China
3.	Shaanxi earthquake	Shaanxi Province, China
4.	Bhola cyclone	Bangladesh
5.	India cyclone	India
6.	Antioch earthquake	Antioch, Byzantine Empire
7.	Tangshan earthquake	Tangshan, Hebei, China
8.	Haiyuan earthquake	Haiyuan, Ningxia-Gansu, China
9.	Indian Ocean earthquake/tsunami	Indian Ocean
10.	Banqiao Dam flood	Zhumadian, Henan Province, China

Deadliest natural disasters by type of event

Type	Event
Avalanche	Wellington avalanche
Blizzard	Iran blizzard
Drought	Great Famine of 1876–78
Earthquake	Shaanxi earthquake
Flood	China floods
Hailstorm	Roopkund, Uttaranchal
Heat wave	European heat wave
Landslide	Vargas mudslides
Limnic eruption	Lake Nyos
Pandemic	Spanish influenza
Tornado	Saturia-Manikganj Sadar tornado
Tropical cyclone	Bhola cyclone
Tsunami	Indian Ocean tsunami
Volcano	Mount Tambora
Wildfire	Peshtigo Fire

Date	Death toll (estimate)
July–November, 1931	1,000,000–4,000,000
September–October, 1887	900,000–2,000,000
23 January 1556	830,000
13 November 1970	500,000
25 November 1839	300,000
20 May 526	250,000
28 July 1976	242,000
26 December 1920	240,000
26 December 2004	230,000
7 August 1975	90,000–230,000

Location	Date	Death toll (estimate)
United States	1 March 1910	96
Iran	February 1972	4000
India	1876–1878	25,250,000
China	23 January 1556	830,000
China	1931	2,000,000–4,000,000
India	Ninth century	200–600
Europe	June–August 2003	37,451
Venezuela	December 1999	20,006
Cameroon	21 August 1986	1746
Worldwide	1918–1920	750,000,000-100,000,000
Bangladesh	26 April 1989	1300
Bangladesh	13 November 1970	200,000–500,000
Indian Ocean	26 December 2004	230,000
Indonesia	1815	92,000
United States	8 October 1871	2000

Ten deadliest earthquakes

Rank	Event	Location
1.	Shaanxi earthquake	China
2.	Tangshan earthquake	China
3.	Haiyuan earthquake	China
4.	Aleppo earthquake	Syria
5.	Indian Ocean earthquake/ tsunami	Indonesia, Sri Lanka, India, Thailand
6.	Damghan earthquake	Iran
7.	Ardabil earthquake	Iran
8.	Hokkaido earthquake	Japan
9.	Ashgabat earthquake	Turkmenistan
10.	Great Kanto earthquake	Japan

Ten deadliest tsunamis

Rank	Event	Location
1.	Indian Ocean tsunami	Indian Ocean
2.	Lisbon earthquake/ tsunami/fire	Portugal, Spain, Morocco, Ireland, England
3.	Messina earthquake/tsunami	Messina, Italy
4.	Krakatoa eruption	Indonesia
5.	tsunami	Tokaido/Nankaido, Japan
6.	tsunami	Japan
7.	Arica earthquake/tsunami	Arica, Chile
8.	Meiji-Sanriku earthquake	Sanriku, Japan
9.	Mount Unzen eruption in southwest Kyushu	Kyushu, Japan
10.	Ryukyu Trench	Japan

Date	Death toll
1556	830,000
1976	255,000
1920	240,000
1138	230,000
2004	230,000
856	200,000
893	150,000
1730	137,000
1948	110,000
1923	105,000

Date	Death toll
2004	230,000
1755	100,000
1908	100,000
1883	36,000
1707	30,000
1826	27,000
1868	25,674
1896	22,070
1792	15,030
1771	13,486

Index